The Collectible

Maxfield Parrish

With Value Guide

William Holland & Douglas Congdon-Martin

Schiffer Publishing Ltd

77 Lower Valley Road, Atglen, PA 19310

Published by Schiffer Publishing, Ltd.
77 Lower Valley Road
Atglen, PA 19310
Please write for a free catalog.
This book may be purchased from the publisher.
Please include $2.95 postage.
Try your bookstore first.

We are interested in hearing from authors
with book ideas on related subjects.

Printed in the United States of America.
ISBN: 0-88740-536-3

Foreword

This book is for collectors of Maxfield Parrish's art work. They have a long and rich history. Almost from the beginning Parrish's work struck a chord with people, causing them to hold onto the beautiful images, and treat them as the art they were.

Some of these people, of course, were able to buy the original drawings and oil paintings which Parrish created, and some few still are, on those rare occasions when they come on the market. Most people, then and now, had to settle for the art as it was reproduced in books, magazines, calendars, art prints, and a myriad of other forms.

This book is for those collectors. It catalogs the public forms that Parrish's art took, and does so to an extent beyond anything previously published. With over 770 full color photographs, it offers an almost complete representation of the published images of Maxfield Parrish.

The Collectible Maxfield Parrish owes a great debt to its predecessors, particularly Coy Ludwig's *Maxfield Parrish*. Originally published in 1973, and recently republished by Schiffer Publishing, Atglen, Pennsylvania, it remains the authority on the life and work of Parrish. Besides being a source of general knowledge, Ludwig's work has provided the basic organization for this current volume. Not only was it difficult to improve on his work, by following the same general order of presentation, the two books work together for cross-referencing.

Among the contributions Ludwig made to Parrish scholarship was the continuation of a numbering system for images that Parrish himself began. Parrish started at number one and continued to 520, which he reached in January, 1910. Ludwig continued the system, assigning numbers to previously unnumbered images, and to those created after 1909. Each image received one number, and that number stayed with it no matter where the image was used. This creates a wonderful reference system, particularly when Parrish's images appear in many forms. The *Parrish/Ludwig* numbering system appears in the "Catalog of Selected Works" which appears at the end of his book (pages 205-219)

The *Parrish/Ludwig Number* appears at the end of each caption in *The Collectible Maxfield Parrish*. We have not presumed to assign numbers to those images that either Parrish or Ludwig did not treat, so those few images are simply designated as "not assigned."

We hope you enjoy reading and using this book. While it is as complete as we could make it at this point, we are eager to locate missing items for the next edition. Please contact us through the publisher.

William R. Holland & Douglas L. Congdon-Martin

Acknowledgements

The publication of this book is a result of some very devoted collectors of Maxfield Parrish images, who were extremely generous with the authors.

Ed Meschi of New Jersey was among the first to embrace the project. A collector and international dealer in Parrish, he shared some of his items with us, and offered us encouragement as we proceeded.

In Ohio, Gary Sample opened his home and his collection to us, and shared his deep love of Parrish's art. This is even more significant in light of Gary's own considerable talent as a commercial artist and illustrator.

Also in Ohio, we met John Crawford who brought pieces from his collection to Gary's home to be included in the book.

As often happens in such a project as this, one path leads to another. Gary Sample introduced us to John Walkowiak, of Minnesota, who kindly took two days from his job to work even harder with us, as we photographed his very extensive collection. It makes up a large part of this volume.

Marvin Mitchell and the Balliol Corporation of Lancaster, Pennsylvania, a friend from other book projects, helped find some of the images that eluded us. He introduced us to Richard Kravitz and Jason Karp.

Art from the archives of Brown & Bigelow Inc.

As always the gathering of materials for an art reference book requires a lot of help and trust. When the work is as extensive as this is, the involvement of others is even more crucial. We are thankful for all those who so willingly shared of themselves in this endeavor, and hope they are gratified with the result of their effort.

Contents

Maxfield Parrish
As His Contemporaries Saw Him

Very often an artist does not live to see his work appreciated by the world. "The struggling artist" is a character of fact and fiction, waiting in poverty to be discovered...a change in the public perception that usually seems to occur soon after the artist dies.

Maxfield Parrish was one of the blessed few who won public recognition and acceptance from the beginning. While he did struggle financially around the turn of the century, this was primarily due to the tuberculosis he contracted at that time, and as he recovered, so did his fortunes. Maxfield Parrish's art caught the public imagination. To name one thing about it that was so captivating would be inaccurate. Rather it was a combination of beautiful colors, skillful drawings, fanciful worlds and creatures to inhabit them, and through it all a humorous yet human approach to life. In the mix was the wonder and magic of Maxfield Parrish, which has made him one of the best loved and most enduring artists of the twentieth century.

Throughout his life, Maxfield parrish was a most reluctant subject of curiosity and fame. While by all accounts he was outgoing and witty and a master of the social graces, he clung strongly to his privacy. Only occasionally do we get a glimpse of the man from his contemporaries, critics and friends, but when we do they are insightful of the artist and his work.

One of the earliest articles about Parrish appeared in *The Red Letter* magazine in 1897. Entitled "A Clever Master of the Grotesque," it was written by Harry D. Hunt. Parrish's "Humpty Dumpty" had appeared the previous December in the magazine, and he was receiving recognition for the covers he was creating at the time for *Harper's.*

At this time Parrish's reputation in poster design had grown to the point where he was known as the "American Poster Competition Winner." His Columbia bicycle poster, designed for Pope Manufacturing Co., won first place in April, 1896, besting at least 525 other entries. That same year he had won a contest for a Hornsby's Oatmeal (H.O.) poster, and received second place in the *Century Midsummer Holiday Number, August* poster contest. In this last contest he competed against 700 other artists, finishing second to another great American illustrator, J.C. Leyendecker. First place might have belonged to Parrish if he had stayed within the rules of the

Amateur photograph of the young Maxfield Parrish.

competition which called for an image that could be printed in three press runs. His required five, according to Ludwig (*Maxfield Parrish* Schiffer Publishing, 1993), but in any case it was published as a poster by the Century Company in 1897.

His success as a poster artist aside, Parrish was gaining most recognition from his cover designs. According to Hunt, in *The Red Letter* article:

His work is always characterized by the same men with attenuated members, decidedly irregular features, and a world of expression in their bead-like eyes and pursed-up cheeks. Mr. Parrish can suggest more by a few dotes and dashes than most men can convey by the most elaborate portrait work. Taken out from the drawings, a series of the mouths, eyes, and noses of his men would look like a shorthand alphabet, but in their proper places they are the most expressive features imaginable.

This was written when Parrish was twenty-six years old. Prophetically, Hunt concludes the article by saying, "Although imminently successful in whatever work he has undertaken, it is mainly in the future that we look to see Mr. Parrish's best work. A young man, his work has the faults of young men, and at the same time their freshness and crispness."

The *Book Buyer* of April, 1898 ran a quite complimentary article about Parrish. Written by James B. Carrington, this, too, is an early critique of the young Parrish, who was established as an illustrator, but still forging a niche in the art world. The best of American illustrators, says Carrington, are first of all painters, "who have learned to adjust their art to the particular demands of drawing for reproduction, and at the same time kept a firm hold upon their sense and appreciation of the picturesque." When these attributes are in evidence, the artists illustrative work has "life" and "snap" to it. Carrington suggests that these qualities separate the artist's work from the work of the camera, which was then threatening to send many illustrators into unemployment.

Carrington writes:

No observer of Mr. Parrish's work can have failed to appreciate the beauty of his line. It is full of delicacy and grace, combined with a sureness of touch that is convincing, and reveals the thorough workman in everything he does...In the drawings that accompanied Mr. Kenneth Grahame's Golden Age story, "Its Walls Were as of Jasper," and later in those illustrating "Mother Goose in Prose," these qualities are shown. In them, too, Mr. Parrish's fine sense of humor is exhibited and his faculty of taking the serious point of view toward his characters that contribute so much to their attraction. It is difficult to recall other illustrations in this vein that are at once so good in themselves and so perfectly in keeping with the written words.

Carrington cites one last quality of Parrish's work: his use of color. "Parrish's use of color has been sometimes compared with Boutet de Monvel's, in that both get their effects by the use of simple flat tints, but I feel justified in saying that Mr. Parrish's methods are the outcome of his own innate and natural instinct for color. That his color sense is highly developed is plainly shown in all his painting, and his fondness for low rich tones and delicate harmonies is but a natural expression of his own refined individuality."

There are few personal facts shared in this early biography by Carrington. We learn that Parrish was from old Quaker stock, that his father was Stephen Parrish, an artist of note. We are told that he attended Haverford College, studied at the Pennsylvania Academy of the Fine Arts in Philadelphia, and entered a class of Howard Pyle at Drexel Institute. We learn that his studio in Philadelphia was a "workmanlike" place and that Parrish enjoyed building things for studio and home.

To today's reader, this is a frustratingly sparse biography. We wish to know as much as possible about those people we admire. The lack of personal information reflects the man. As Carrington concludes the article, "Mr. Parrish holds the creed that the man's work is himself, and his own work bears the mark of sincerity and directness that belong to the man."

Parrish's early studio in Philadelphia.

We get further insight into Parrish's thoughts and work from a letter he wrote to Orson Lowell, shortly after the *Book Buyer* article appeared. It was written from The Oaks, Parrish's home and studio in Cornish, New Hampshire (its post office was in Windsor, Vermont) on May 2, 1898, the spring when he was deeply involved in the design and building of his home there.

Dear Sir: I have just read your letter and wish to thank you for your request. I hope you will not think me disobliging, or fussy, or peculiar; but really I *don't* want anything written about me. There are ever so many reasons why not—too many for modesty to find a place—and "The Book Buyer" has just had an article which should undoubtedly last for a long time to come. I have never cared anything about my posters or other commercial work, and know that the less said about them the better. And if there is one thing above all others which is awful, it is the modern tendency to want to know 'how he came to do it.' But I thank you for taking so much interest in me and hope you will understand. Sincerely, Maxfield Parrish.

Lowell was not alone in the interest he had in Parrish. The images Parrish created caught the public's imagination.

The first book to contain Parrish's illustrations in full-color was Eugene Field's *Poems of Childhood.* It was published in September, 1904, and represented a comeback, of sorts, for Parrish. Stricken with tuberculosis in 1900, he spent two years recovering, first at Saranac Lake, New York, then at Castle Creek, Hot Springs, Arizona. He continued to create during this time, but his work slowed.

The appearance of *Poems of Childhood* was hailed as an important literary and artistic event. William D. Moffat, writing in the December 3, 1904 issue of *The Outlook,* said that it stirred "anew the enthusiasm that this artist's work almost invariably arouses."

Moffat makes special note of Parrish's color work. He reflects on Parrish's cover designs, which he calls "exquisite" and "poetic" and the source of Parrish's fame. "His fine decorative effects in deep purple forest or sunny blue sky in delicately modeled figures or formal classic architecture, were something new in the art of cover designing, and they became standards of beauty of their kind."

Looking at *Poems of Childhood,* Moffat notes the humor in Parrish's work, calling it "delicious" and of "the finest kind." He notes, however, that "the humorist in him is balanced by the poet, and frequently the two are exquisitely combined. The poetic vein in his nature is exalted and spiritual, the humor quaint and whimsical." Both are found in the *Poems of Childhood.*

And they are found in color. "Mr. Parrish is at his best in color," writes Moffat. "His palette is rich and full; his use of color strikingly effective, both a means of artistic and of poetic expression." He notes the power of the works: the "splendidly somber shadows wherein the child-imagination expands" in "The Sugar-Plum Tree"; the "pale mists" and "wonderful sights" of "Wynken, Blynken, and Nod"; the "most actual and realistic" figures of "Little John and his Sister Sue". "Seein' Things at Night" writes Moffat, "is a composition...that no child can look upon with composure. The foreground of the picture shows Mr. Parrish in his most careful mood, working out with amazing technique the folds and squared pattern of the fabric."

Moffat's highest praise was saved for "The Dinkey Bird," which he calls the most beautiful and poetic of all the compositions in the book.

It seems to us that Mr. Parrish has made no illustration more exquisitely charming than this, in color, in composition, and in poetic feeling. With the picture before us we read the poem again and find new meanings in it. It is more than an illustration; it is an illuminating interpretation. One can linger long over these pictures and come back to them eagerly after laying them down.

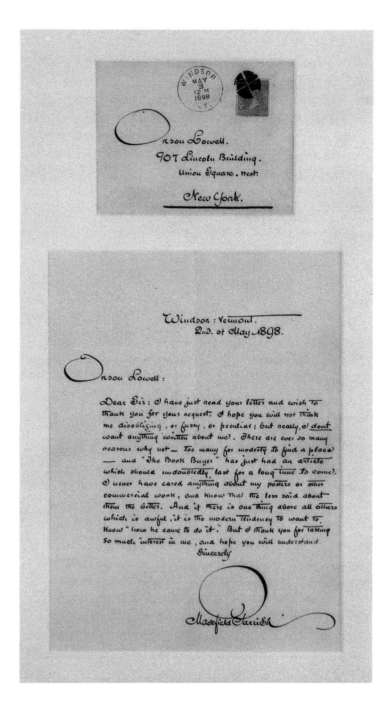

Parrish wrote this letter to Orson Lowell of New York on May 2, 1898. It is in response to a request for an interview.

The color illustrations that appeared in books, on posters, and in the magazines of the late nineteenth and early twentieth centuries were highly valued by the public. Color lithography, introduced in the mid-nineteenth century, had slowly developed to the point where an image could be produced with high quality in an economical manner. Magazines began to appear with color covers and illustrations, and the public went on a color "frenzy" during the last two decades of the 1800s. People cherished the color images, preserving and saving them, and oftentimes, placing them in frames to decorate the walls of their homes.

Into this world stepped the talented Parrish, whose whimsical, romantic images, and strong sense of color composition, were precisely what the public desired.

It is probably for this reason that "The Dinkey Bird" remains a favorite of Parrish collectors to this day.

Parrish was only a little over thirty years old when Moffat wrote this review. As he notes, there had always been a maturity to Parrish's work, as though he "had never...had term of apprenticeship, but...arrived full-fledged and finished in his art." Nevertheless, in concluding the piece, Moffat hints at the future of the artist: "Each new work of his is in a way a new revelation, and it would be hard to fix the limit of his power."

A more intimate look at Parrish was written by Homer Saint-Gaudens, a fellow resident of the artistic community of Cornish, New Hampshire, a contemporary of Parrish's, and the son of the sculptor, Augustus Saint-Gaudens. Writing in the June, 1905 issue of *The Critic*, he recounts tales from Parrish's childhood, telling how his first aspiration was to be a carpenter, and then, "such is the vacillation of youth, a soda-fountain man where he might shine up the nickel-work." Early on he began to embellish his autograph with architectural designs. He, along with two "boy-cousins" lived in a "world of cut-out paper things, such as knights in armor with suits to take off and put on, and plenty of bad people, because one of the boys could imitate the gushing of blood to a tee. So when they got tired of a certain character, or he became shopworn, they erected a guillotine, and his head was taken off, while the blood gushed, so that they had to roll up what trousers they had on." The cut-outs had a more serious purpose as he matured. He used them to construct his work and set the forms of his characters.

Saint-Gaudens describes in some depth the design and building of the Oaks, paying particular attention to the details of decor and furnishings. He also notes, as do others, the extensive workshop Parrish had at The Oaks. Having begun the article with a quotation from Parrish's father, Stephen, that "Fred [Maxfield] is more of an artisan than an artist," Saint-Gaudens stresses the importance of Parrish's technical skill and knowledge of materials. "Shopwork often goes hand in hand with painting. To get a vase or a column or a fountain with a certain shadow the object is turned out, placed in the proper light,—and there you are...Few artists are such good artisans."

Saint-Gaudens continues:

...At Cornish he has generated that particular fashion of handling oils, and black and white, not only of intrinsic worth but adaptable to decoration, to poster and book-cover designing, and to illustrating; in which latter province he most skilfully copes with the difficulties of color reproduction. Best of all, he has mastered the power of mingling work and play in the expression of his buoyant good humor. Scarcely a letter or an envelope goes from his hand unembellished...Never did

Parrish's workshop at The Oaks, in Cornish, New Hampshire.

a man, his home, his amusements, and his vocation appear in happier accord...

Parrish imparts to each composition many delicate details ever subordinated and in harmony; since with all their finished execution his results are never trivial, cramped, stiff, or labored, but retain where needed a sweet fresh movement...These very details carried to a higher power, together with a fondness for children, have augmented his grotesque humor of treating comic characters seriously...This whimsical sense of fun runs through Parrish's whole life, for rarely is a sentence spoken untouched by his gentle wit and odd sentiment. And his very human interest in the round world instils with a human element the most fantastic examples of his work.

Saint-Gaudens goes on to laud his friend's work for its graceful lines, the use of figures in the composition, and its rendering of light and shadow.

But in his conclusion, he reveals the same frustration that Parrish himself spoke of in his letter to Mr. Lowell, some seven years before. Despite his extreme popularity as an illustrator, he is not satisfied. He longs toward painting, but "he has not yet entered the field...He progresses with deliberate purpose and power that seems to aim at mural decoration with his taste for architectural effects."

Parrish's longing was supported by at least one art authority of the day. Professor Hubert Von Herkomer's opinion of Parrish was the subject of an article by J.H. Irvine in the July, 1906 issue of *The International Studio*.

Quite by chance, Von Herkomer had received a copy of a leaflet which contained a reproduction of the frontispiece of *The Golden Age*. Though illustrators were generally considered somewhat beneath the talent and respect accorded to "fine" artists, Von Herkomer was so impressed by the quality of Parrish's work that he was moved to write to the publisher, John Lane. The letter is quoted in Irvine's article: "Mr. Parrish has absorbed, yet purified, every modern oddity, and added to it his own strong original identity. He has combined the photographic vision with the pre-Raphaelite feeling. He is poetic without ever being maudlin, and has the saving clause of humour. He can give suggestiveness without loss of unflinching detail. He has a strong sense of romance. He has a great sense of characterization without a touch of ugliness. He can be modern, medieval, or classic. He has been able to infuse into the mose uncompromising realism the decorative element—an extraordinary feat in itself. He is throughout and excellent draughtsman, and his finish is phenomenal. Altogether this original artist is the strangest mixture I have ever met with. This man should paint, and not lose himself for the art world by merely doing illustrations. He will do much to reconcile the extreme and sober elements of our times."

Such praise based on a pamphlet! The compliments continue as Irvine interviews Von Herkomer about Parrish. While it is doubtful that Von Herkomer knew about Parrish's extensive use of photograph in producing his images, he insightfully makes the connection.

...one of the most interesting things about him is just the admixture of the camera-esque and the picturesque. Without sacrificing a single artist virtue that was in recognized existence before the advent of photography, his work seems nevertheless to recognize the fact that photography has come and intends to remain.

Referring to the image of the gardener shaking his fist in *Dream Days*, he continues

Would anyone have drawn trees as in this illustration without having seen them through the mechanical representation of the camera? But the 'geist' of the man knows with unfailing taste when to introduce that aspect.

Von Herkomer's feeling about Parrish is clear when he tells Irvine, "It is a comfort to know of a man existing in our age of abnormal haste who will so deliberately work out his thoughts, sparing neither time nor labour in order to express wholly his designs."

As the recognition of his talent and the respect he received from his peers grew, so did his popularity with the public. His illustrations were found more and more widely in magazines, books, and advertisements. Then, in 1911, he received a commission for a series of eighteen murals for the girls' dining room at the Curtis Publishing Company headquarters in Philadelphia. It was a mammoth undertaking, both in scope and in the size of the paintings. Each was more than 10 feet tall.

Curtis Publishing was not shy about publicizing the event, and used images from the murals in a variety of ways, from subscription cards to magazine covers. The exposure brought Parrish to a new level of public recognition and fame.

A humorous tribute to Maxfield Parrish was made in this cartoon appearing in *Life*, entitled "Popular Illustrators at Work: Maxfield Parrish."

In 1912, his friend and college classmate, Christian Brinton, published a recollection of Parrish for *The Century* magazine. In "A Master of Make-Believe" he relates some of the same stories Saint-Gaudens had told earlier about the childhood of Parrish, then gives some of the details of Parrish's years at Haverford College. He tells of the wonders of Parrish's suite at Barclay Hall, transformed with paint, crayon, chalk and a variety of found objects into a place of enchantment.

So awestruck were the Philistines by this array of taste that they would pause transfixed upon the threshold, not presuming to enter without a condescending nod from one or other of the occupants. And when it came to the wild, nocturnal carnival of hazing an room-wrecking, it was a recognized tradition that this particular suite must remain inviolate.

Brinton saw in Parrish a kind of magical power of creativity. That power was brought to bear on Cornish when he moved his home and studio there. "Cornish may have existed before his advent," writes Brinton, but there "are grounds for doubting this and every reason for affirming that, aesthetically, he remade Cornish, just as years before he remade his rooms at college. After his coming, folk began remarking that the hills seemed to shape and group themselves more effectively, that certain trees stood forth more picturesquely against the horizon, and that those swift-scudding cloud-forms marshaled themselves almost as majestically across the sky as they did in the backgrounds of his canvases."

Moving to the present Brinton described the recently finished murals at Curtis Publishing.

The scheme represents, with characteristic flexibility as to details and treatment, a Venetian fete, and in this serenely gay processional, which runs around three sides of the room, are grouped most of his favorite scenes or personages. It is in a sense an epitome in line and tone of his entire artistic career. There are cavaliers and grand ladies galore; there are serenades and surprises; there are lovelorn misses, pages, and laughing coquettes;there are broad terraces and slender, soaring columns, great, flowered vases, and dark cedar boughs sweeping full across skies suffused with the amber and gold of sunset. The effect is cumulative. He has here had the space to unite all those frankly happy creatures with whom he has lived so long, and never have they seemed so radiant and care-free. Never have they appeared so imbued with beauty or touched with poetic sentiment.

For this book about collecting Maxfield Parrish, it is interesting to note that Brinton finishes his article with a word about the home of the Austin M. Purveses of Chestnut Hill, Pennsylvania. He describes this place, crowded with Parrish's work, as the only place where "you can get on intimate terms with him."

One of the more helpful insights to Parrish's gift comes from Adeline Adams writing in the *American Magazine of Art* for January, 1918. His grand Curtis murals behind him, it is possible for Adams to see Parrish not only as illustrator waiting to become a painter, but as a genius whose strongest characteristic is "his manysidedness in art." She writes, "...he believes that the painter's art is not necessarily a mere business of likenesses, landscapes, genre pictures, mural decorations. He sees it as something bigger and broader, something that is good for homely as well as for exalted purposes, something that shall envelop and enrich all human life, every-day fripperies included... He is unique in his universality."

If she accurately captured Parrish's thinking, it had surely moved a great distance from the thoughts contained in the letter to Mr. Lowell some twenty years before. Here we see a mature artist, who has come to terms with all aspects of his work.

Adams shares the implications of Parrish's artistic integrity:

His artistic conscience, together with his felicity of conception and his mastery of his materials, delivers out of the commonplace every poster and advertisement coming from his hand. An advertisement for chocolate cannot be prosaic and stodgy if given the poetry of his composition and color, with a happy touch of raillery to help the world along. The thing is very simple. Why should he let his art be dragged down by the other man's chocolate, when after all, the contract was that he should life up the other man's chocolate by his art? He would tell you so himself, if he were not constitutionally incapable of self-righteous sayings. His recent poster showing a varlet astride an automobile tire, and racing from one glorious end of the Sierras to the other [Fisk Tire advertisement], is as truly in the grand style as if it had been planned as a decoration for the Supreme Court.

A few years since, some one was grumbling because in order to see a Parrish mural decoration, he had to go gayly to a bar, or sedately to a club. Old King Cole reigned at the Knickerbocker Hotel in New York, while the panel lettered Quod Erat Demonstrandum is at the Meeting House Club in New York. Today examples are less scarce. The Ladies' Home Journal Building has an important series in which certain very difficult problems of space and lighting are solved. Bright throngs of figures, high-keyed to their business of happiness and evidently "all dressed up, somewhere to go," pass and repass through stately gardens, rich with leafage and classic vases, seen against sunset hills. The almost inexhaustible wealth of lovely detail is balanced by large free spaces. A ponderous visitor once asked Mr. Parrish "whether the work represented one of those care-free pageants so eminently characteristic of aristocratic existence at the height of the Italian Renaissance," "To be sure," answered the artist, after a pause in deference to profundity, "Just some people going to a party."

This accessibility of Parrish contributed, no doubt, to his popularity. The images he created, whether comic or simply beautiful, required no degree in art history or criticism to understand and be appreciated. He brought his vast skill and vision and creative magic to the canvas or the paper, from which emerged an image that spoke to the common person.

The democratic spirit of Parrish's artistic concerns extends at least to his sixtieth year. An interview with M.K. Wisehart appeared in the *American Magazine* in

May, 1930. Still reluctant to speak with the press, Parrish tried to put off Wisehart at least until spring. He was surprised, yet cordial, when the reporter showed up at his door.

As the interview proceeds, Wisehart turns to Parrish's life, summarizing his childhood, his college years and his early career. Finally he asks Parrish to reflect on the first forty years of a wonderfully successful professional life. "I should like to know what this means to you as you think of it today. What have you got out of it so far?"

"In answer," says Wisehart, "he told me why the first forty years are the hardest." He goes on to paraphrase Parrish's reflections.

In the beginning, one does what he can, and should, and must. One is apt to drift. That is one way of working out the great major problems of life. It is not always well to try to go against the current. There are times when it is best to go with it. During the forty years' epoch you have certain problems to solve. Though these may not be the problems you are most interested in solving, it is for you to get out of them all of which you are capable.

He continues:

During the epoch when he was doing what needed to be done, Mr. Parrish put so much into his work and got so much out of the problems to be solved, that he became known as America's foremost illustrator-artist, and one of the finest colorists we have produced. Prints of his work have sold by the hundreds of thousands. He beautifully illustrated many wonderful murals. He became financially independent. Today, he can pick his own problems and solve them in his own way. This is the goal at which the artist can arrive if the first forty years go well!

Parrish was sixty years old when this interview took place. At about the time most people consider retirement, he was about to enter a new phase in his career. He told Wisehart that he thought of himself as being at the beginning of his career. "He will tell you that he no longer chooses to paint what might be regarded as a mere portrait of the out-of-doors. He seeks to express what gives him personally his greatest joy—the effects of light and character, space and air, the quality of things."

Six years later, Parrish was exhibiting at the Ferargil Gallery on 17th Street in New York City. An article in *Time*, February 17, 1936, reports that he was received with great acclaim. "No matter what art critics may think," the article reported, "art dealers know that, as far as the sale of expensive art reproductions is concerned, the three most popular artists in the world are Van Gogh, Cézanne, and Maxfield Parrish."

The *Time* article quotes Charles Fabens Kelley of the Chicago Art Institute as commenting that Parrish has no imitators because "it is just too darned hard work to imitate him...he can domesticate the most unruly colors."

As for his new beginning, we are told that though the pictures were all new, he kept to his old style: "pink rocks in a blue mist, spinach-green trees in a theatrical amber light, all ticked out in the most minute detail. True to his promise five years ago to paint no more nude girls on rocks, there are no figure studies in the present exhibition."

One last commentary on Parrish and his significance is interesting to note. It comes from Julie Nixon Eisenhower writing in *The Saturday Evening Post*, in December, 1974. Coy Ludwig's biography of Maxfield Parrish had recently been published, and there was a rebirth of popularity of the artist. Capitalizing on this, *The Saturday Evening Post* cleverly called the article, "The Outer Space Beauty of Maxfield Parrish," though Eisenhower never uses the phrase to describe Parrish's work. She is captivated by the unreality of his work, the "unearthly" colors, the magical room to dream that Parrish's art provides.

December, 1974 was a time of crisis and turmoil for the nation and for its former leader, Richard Nixon. He had resigned from office on August 9th of that year, and the nation was still reeling from the unprecedented history that had unfolded before it. As a member of the President's family, Eisenhower doubtless felt a great depth of pain in a most personal way.

She found in Parrish some relief, which she welcomed personally, and offered to the nation. "Maxfield Parrish," she wrote, "stands out today because of the joy and fullness of life embodied in his paintings. The theatrical settings, the escapist themes, the vibrancy and sheer beauty of his rich colors, and the dreamlike sensuousness of some of his work—all of these qualities make his art unique. Unusual and different at the turn of the century. Unusual and different, and, perhaps, needed as a ray of joy today."

Each generation has found for itself the beauty of Parrish's art, the delight and joy it can bring, and the power it has to awaken the imagination and give space and time to fancy and fantasy. It is this discovery, time after time, generation after generation, that has kept collectors clamoring for Parrish's work to adorn their homes. They have kept the wonder alive.

For The Collector

What to Collect

Maxfield Parrish was prolific. Perhaps there are so many Parrish collectors because there is so much to collect.

The Parrish collector will want to have expansive wall space, a few showcases and at least one large bookcase. Start by filling the walls with art prints; maybe a separate room for the Brown & Bigelow calendars, and one for your favorite magazine covers. You will need a super special spot for those rare, early posters—but not in direct sunlight. In the showcase you will put some decks of playing cards, Murphy thermometers, and E-M tape measure, maybe a Parker Brother's game and some Crane chocolate boxes. Put the Mazda light bulb display on the end table. Finally fill the bookcase with all your favorite Parrish illustrated books.

That was fun. Now let's go back one step.

Finding Maxfield Parrish

Auctions, flea markets, mail order, general antique dealers, Parrish specialists. These main sources for Parrish collectibles should pass three tests in order to become worthy recipients of your hard-earned dollars.

The person must be *knowledgeable* of Maxfield Parrish items. He or she should be able to separate the original from the reprints, explain foxing and fading, and give you valuable information on rarity, size differences, relative prices and market trends.

The person must be *reputable*. A reputable dealer will not misrepresent age, condition, or origin of anything he or she sells. A reputable person will stand behind his or her merchandise—guaranteeing authenticity in writing and offering to "take it back" if there is any complaint.

The person must be *available*. Later on, if you cannot find the dealer, then you will have a difficult time resolving any questions or disputes.

When you find a dealer with all three attributes, rejoice, for you will always have peace of mind concerning your purchases.

Judging Condition

Paper is a very delicate material. Magazine covers were printed on cheap acidic paper and were especially prone to damage and deterioration. The calendars were give-away items, also printed on acidic paper or cardboard.

Most were used and then discarded. Those that survived were relegated to the box of old papers in the closet or attic, where silverfish, mice, and accumulated dirt have taken their toll. Even worse are those items stored in a damp and sometimes flooded basement.

Framed items, like the art prints, have also suffered from improper storage. On the walls another enemy was silently at work—light. Parrish was very demanding of his printers. He insisted that they use all their abilities to bring out his beautiful colors when making a print from his original oil painting. The results were the vivid and striking prints that we value so greatly. Unfortunately, he exercised no control over the handling and framing of the prints after their creation.

Most were framed unmatted, with the print pressed directly against the glass. Many were dry-mounted or backed with acidic cardboard as well. Today the effect of years of sunlight is noticeable on many Parrish art prints. The pink flowers and bright yellow sunlight are gone from many, many "Daybreaks". The girl in "Stars" has an unusual green skin tone. The red-brown leaves in "Hilltop" and "The Lute Players" have faded to a muddy green. Ironically, some collectors actually like the muted tones on some prints better than the strong colors of an unfaded version.

There are prints, calendars, and magazine covers with exceptional color available to the collector who is willing to pay for top quality. Since condition is the main price determinant, sometimes you can pick up a rare piece at an affordable price if you can accept it being less than mint. Fading, minor creases and small foxing spots are usually not too objectionable. Tears and holes should greatly reduce the price and pieces with them should be only a temporary addition to your collection until a better example comes along. Bad water stains are most unsightly, acceptable only to the most forgiving collector.

The art prints are most desirable in their original frames. Period frames are acceptable at a slightly lower price. If you find a great print in a new frame, plan on upgrading the frame when one becomes available. Calendars and magazine covers are preferred framed in old frames. New frames are acceptable if done in the traditional Parrish style. Part of the fun of collecting is finding the items of your dreams, and it is just as gratifying to seek out and find better examples and "trade up."

Price

Price guides, including the one for this book, can be useful in gauging relative values (i.e. "Stars" is worth more than "Daybreak"), and establishing an initial price *range*. The weakness of price guides, especially for Maxfield Parrish items, is the great differences in price depending on condition and on the geographic area where the item is being sold. In coin collecting there is a very specific grading system which every good coin dealer follows. In an ideal world, Parrish items could be graded similarly. Unfortunately, no one has agreed upon a workable system.

Here are some general rules to follow when using price guides.

1. Use price guide values as a starting point only.

2. Compare prices at a number of dealers to see if you are in an above—or below—average demand area.

3. Recognize that prices change, either across the board or on individual pieces and that there is always a time lag between the compiling of the guide and its release to the public.

4. Remember that since there are so many variables concerning condition, each piece must be graded and valued on its own merits (or flaws).

5. When selling, assume that dealers will pay 50-70% of *their* retail—no matter what any guide says the item is worth.

Reproductions

Since the early seventies, copies have been produced of many Parrish art prints, advertisements, posters, and calendar tops. Almost all were printed on a glossy paper which varies greatly from the dull finish of the originals.

Out of the frame, the reproductions are easily identified. Under glass they require a closer scrutiny. The two most obvious differences are coloring and clarity. The reproductions are remarkably colorful, but the colors look artificial and harsh. Because of the cheap printing process, clarity is compromised. The reprints look fuzzy, with the colors blurring together slightly.

Buy only from reputable and knowledgeable sources until you become familiar with the differences. Do not be afraid to purchase a print simply because someone has put new acid-free material behind it. Paper conservators are aghast at the number of collectors who spend hundreds of dollars on a Parrish print and then leave the dirt on the inside of the glass and the acidic cardboard behind it in the frame.

Of course, if you doubt its authenticity of the dealer is unknown and not willing to guarantee it, do not buy it.

Happy hunting!

Book Illustrations

In 1897, Way and Williams of Chicago were preparing to publish a work by a new author, L. Frank Baum. The book was a children's book named *Mother Goose in Prose* and it required some eyecatching illustrations to make it work. They turned to a young artist from Philadelphia, whose cover and illustration work for *Harper's* had won critical and popular acclaim.

Maxfield Parrish's illustrations for *Mother Goose* were a great success, and in the years that followed he created covers and illustrations for a large number of books, most of which are illustrated on the pages that follow. In the early years they were principally reproduced in black and white. With *Poems of Childhood* in 1904, Parrish's work began to be printed in color, and his popularity was boosted even higher. His final book illustrations, for *The Knave of Hearts* published in 1925, are the culmination of his work as an illustrator.

For the collector, it is most desirable to find the illustrations as they were originally intended, bound in a mint condition book. In reality, they are often found excised from the books, and offered as single pages.

The Arabian Nights: Their Best-Known Tales. Edited by Kate Wiggin & Nora Smith, Illustrated by Maxfield Parrish. Parrish did the cover, the end papers, the title page and twelve full color illustrations for this volume. Charles Scribner's Sons, 1909. The cover illustration is "The Fisherman." *Parrish/Ludwig No. 512.*

End papers for *Arabian Nights. Parrish/Ludwig No. 513*

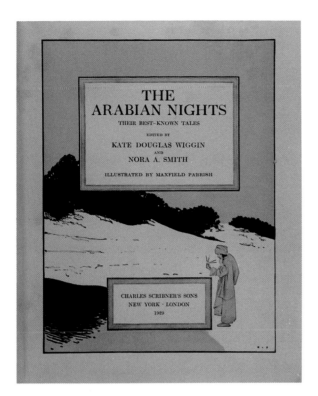

Title page. *Parrish/Ludwig No. 514*

*The smoke ascended to the clouds, and extending itself along
the sea and upon the shore formed a great mist.*

"The Fisherman and the Genie." *Parrish/Ludwig No. 412*

*It will be sufficient to break off a branch and carry it to plant
in your garden.*

"The Talking Bird." *Parrish/Ludwig No. 415*

"The Young King of the Black Isles." *Parrish/Ludwig No. 421*

And she proceeded to burn perfume and repeat spells until the
sea foamed and was agitated.

"Gulnare of the Sea." *Parrish/Ludwig No. 418*

"Prince Agib, Landing of the Brazen Boatman." *Parrish/Ludwig No. 420*

At the same time the earth, trembling, opened just before the
magician, and uncovered a stone, laid horizontally, with
a brass ring fixed into the middle.

At the approach of evening I opened the first closet and,
entering it, found a mansion like paradise.

"Aladdin." *Parrish/Ludwig No. 410*

"Prince Agib, the Story of the King's Son." *Parrish/Ludwig No. 411*

And when they had ascended that mountain they saw a city than which eyes had not beheld any greater.

"The City of Brass." *Parrish/Ludwig No. 417*

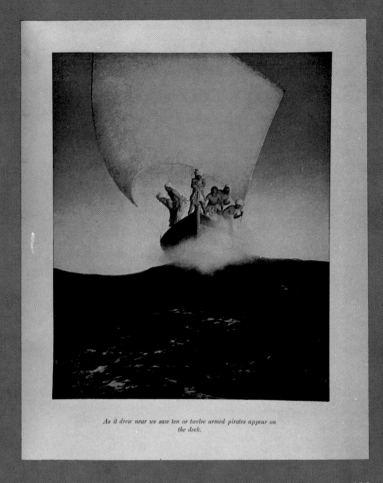

As it drew near we saw ten or twelve armed pirates appear on the deck.

"The History of Codadad and His Brothers." *Parrish/Ludwig No. 419*

Cassim . . . was so alarmed at the danger he was in that the more he endeavored to remember the word Sesame the more his memory was confounded.

"The Story of Ali Baba and the Forty Thieves." *Parrish/Ludwig No. 413*

Having finished his repast, he returned to his porch, where he lay and fell asleep, snoring louder than thunder.

"The Third Voyage of Sinbad." *Parrish/Ludwig No. 414*

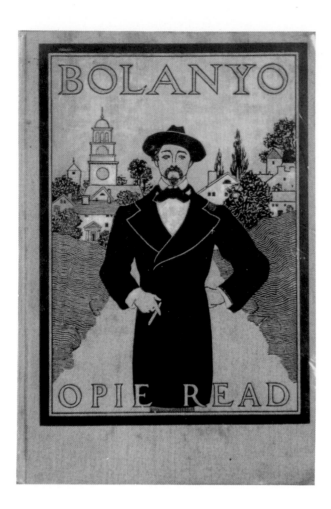

Bolanyo, by Opie Read and published by Way & Williams, 1897. Parrish illustrated the cover. *Parrish/Ludwig No. 093*

Dream Days, by Kenneth Grahame, John Lane Company, 1898. In addition to the cover, Parrish provided ten illustrations in black and white, shown here, and three tailpieces. *Parrish/Ludwig No. 542*

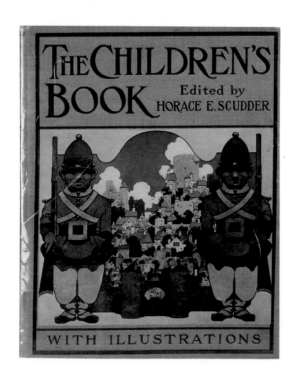

The Children's Book, edited by Horace E. Scudder, Houghton Mifflin Company, 1907. Parrish provided the color cover illustration, "Toyland." *Parrish/Ludwig No. 479*

"Its Walls Were as of Jasper," frontispiece. *Parrish/Ludwig No. 277*

"The Twenty-First of October." *Parrish/ Ludwig No. 543*

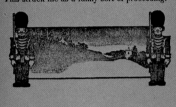

DIES IRÆ

Harold explained, " and the hamper got joggled about on the journey, and the presents worked down into the straw and all over the place. One of 'em turned up inside the cold duck. And that 's why they were n't found at first. And Edward said, Thanks *awfully!*"

I did not see Martha again until we were all re-assembled at tea-time, when she seemed red-eyed and strangely silent, neither scolding nor finding fault with anything. Instead, she was very kind and thoughtful with jams and things, feverishly pressing unwonted delicacies on us, who wanted little pressing enough. Then suddenly, when I was busiest, she disappeared; and Charlotte whispered me presently that she had heard her go to her room and lock herself in. This struck me as a funny sort of proceeding.

Tailpiece for "Dies Irae." *Parrish/ Ludwig No. 546*

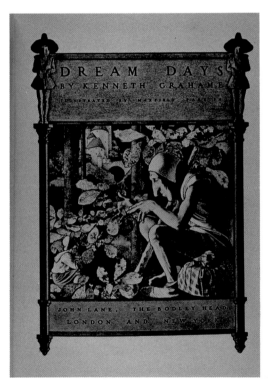

The title page from *Dream Days. Parrish Ludwig No. 276*

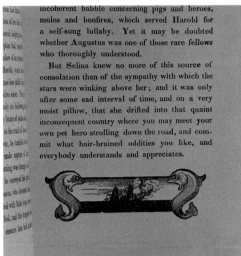

incoherent babble concerning pigs and heroes, moles and bonfires, which served Harold for a self-sung lullaby. Yet it may be doubted whether Augustus was one of those rare fellows who thoroughly understood.

But Selina knew no more of this source of consolation than of the sympathy with which the stars were winking above her; and it was only after some sad interval of time, and on a very moist pillow, that she drifted into that quaint inconsequent country where you may meet your own pet hero strolling down the road, and commit what hair-brained oddities you like, and everybody understands and appreciates.

Tailpiece for "The Twenty First of October." *Parrish/Ludwig No. 544*

"Mutabile Semper." *Parrish/Ludwig No. 297*

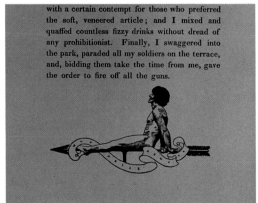

with a certain contempt for those who preferred the soft, veneered article; and I mixed and quaffed countless fizzy drinks without dread of any prohibitionist. Finally, I swaggered into the park, paraded all my soldiers on the terrace, and, bidding them take the time from me, gave the order to fire off all the guns.

Tailpiece for "Mutabile Semper." *Parrish/ Ludwig No. 547*

"Dies Irae." *Parrish/Ludwig No. 545*

"The Magic Ring." *Parrish/Ludwig No. 295*

"A Saga of the Seas." *Parrish/Ludwig No. 298*

"A Departure." *Parrish/Ludwig No. 551*

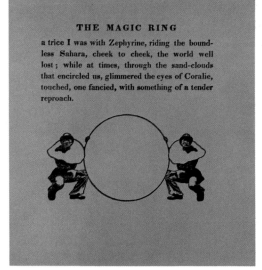

Tailpiece for "The Magic Ring." *Parrish/ Ludwig No. 299*

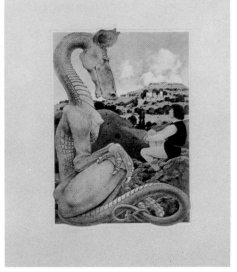

"The Reluctant Dragon." *Parrish/Ludwig No. 549*

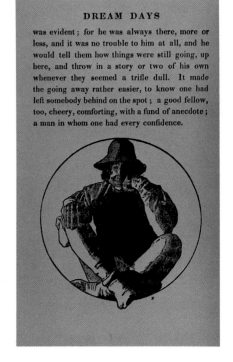

Tailpiece for "The Departure." *Parrish/ Ludwig No. 300*

"Its Walls Were as of Jasper." *Parrish/ Ludwig No. 548*

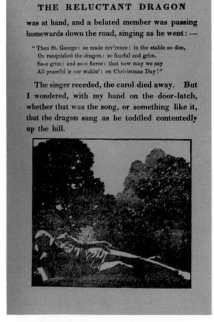

Tailpiece for "The Reluctant Dragon." *Parrish/Ludwig No. 550*

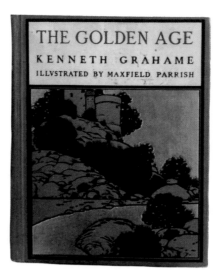

Golden Age, by Kenneth Grahame, with illustrations by Maxfield Parrish. This cover illustration was used on *Dream Days*. The book included nineteen black and white illustrations, and thirteen tailpieces, shown here. John Lane Company, 1899.

Free to Serve, by Emma Rayner, Copeland & Day, 1897. Parrish provided this color cover illustration. *Parrish/Ludwig No. 137*

Cover lining used for *The Golden Age* and for *Dream Days*.

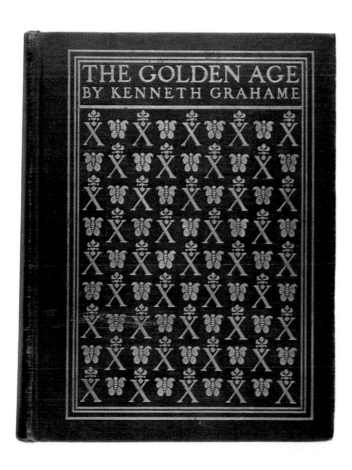

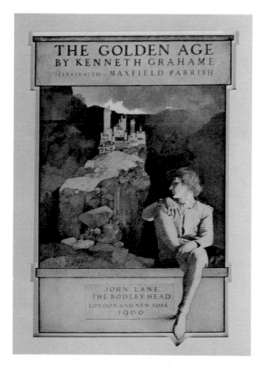

Parrish designed this cover for the first edition of Kenneth Grahame's *The Golden Age*, published by John Lane. *Parrish/Ludwig No. 211*

Title page for *The Golden Age. Parrish/ Ludwig No. 214*

"Onto the garden wall, which led in its turn to the roof of an outhouse," an illustration for "The Burglars," in *The Golden Age. Parrish/Ludwig No. 228*

"Out into the brimming sun-bathed world I sped," illustration for "A Holiday," in *The Golden Age. Parrish/Ludwig No. 222*

"Once more were damsels rescued, dragons disemboweled, and giants...," an illustration for "Alarums and Excursions," in *The Golden Age. Parrish/Ludwig No. 224*

"For them the orchard (a place elf-haunted, wonderful!) simply..." an illustration for "Prologue: The Olympians," in *The Golden Age. Parrish/Ludwig No. 220*

I took the old fellow to the station," illustration for "A White-washed Uncle," in *The Golden Age. Parrish/Ludwig No. 226*

"Lulled by the trickle of water, I slipped into dreamland," from "The Finding of the Princess," in *The Golden Age. Parrish/ Ludwig No. 210*

Tailpiece for "The Olympians." *Parrish/ Ludwig No. 236*

Tailpiece for "Piebald Pig." *Parrish/Ludwig No. 237*

Tailpiece for "Young Adam Cupid." *Parrish/ Ludwig No. 239*

Tailpiece for "Snowbound"." *Parrish/ Ludwig No. 240*

"It was easy...to transport yourself in a trice to the heart of a tropical forest," from "Sawdust and sin" in *The Golden Age. Parrish/Ludwig No. 221*

Tailpiece for "Sawdust and Sin." *Parrish/ Ludwig No. 238*

"A great book open on his knee...a score or so disposed within easy reach," from "A Harvesting" in *The Golden Age. Parrish/ Ludwig No. 225*

"They make me walk behind, 'cos they say I'm too little, and musn't hear," from "What They Talked About" in *The Golden Age. Parrish/Ludwig No. 230*

Tailpiece from "What They Talked About." *Parrish/Ludwig No. 241*

"Who would have thought...that only two short days ago we had confronted each other on either side of a hedge," from "Young Adam Cupid" in *The Golden Age. Parrish/Ludwig No. 227*

"But yester-eve and the mummers were here!" from "Snowbound" in *The Golden Age. Parrish/Ludwig No. 201.*

"I'm Jason...and this the Argo...and we're just hoing through the Hellespont," from "The Argonauts" in *The Golden Age. Parrish/Ludwig No. 231*

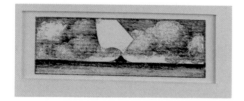

Tailpiece from "The Argonauts." *Parrish/Ludwig No. 242*

"You haven't been to Rome, have you?" from "The Roman Road" in *The Golden Age. Parrish/Ludwig No. 223*

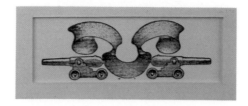

Tailpiece for "The Roman Road." *Parrish/Ludwig No. 243*

"At breakfast Miss Smedley behaved in a most mean and uncalled-for manner," from "Exit Tyrannus" in *The Golden Age. Parrish/Ludwig No. 223*

Tailpiece for "Exit Tyrannus" *Parrish/Ludwig No. 244*

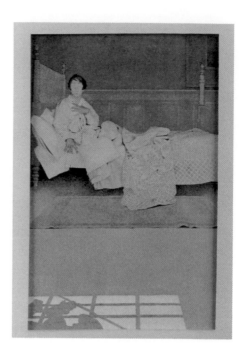

"The procession passing solemnly across the moon-lit Blue Room..." from "The Blue Room" in *The Golden Age. Parrish/Ludwig No. 202*

Tailpiece for "The Blue Room." *Parrish/Ludwig No. 245*

"Why, Master Harold! whatever be the matter? Baint runnin' away be ee?" from "A Falling Out" in *The Golden Age. Parrish/Ludwig No. 203*

Tailpiece for "A Falling Out." *Parrish/ Ludwig No. 246*

"Finally we found ourselves sitting silent on an upturned wheelbarrow," from "Lusisti Satis" in *The Golden Age. Parrish/Ludwig No. 232*

The Golden Treasury of Songs and Lyrics, Duffield & Company, 1911. Although you cannot tell it from the cover, the author is Francis Turner Palgrave. Top billing is given to Parrish who provided eight color illustrations for the 1911 edition. These illustrations originally appeared as *Collier's* covers or illustrations between the years 1904 and 1910, and most can be found with magazine illustrations. They are "Autumn" (10/28/05), "The Lantern Bearers" (12/10/10), "Three Shepherds" (12/3/04), "Summer" (7/22/05), "Harvest" (9/23/05), "Pierrot" (8/8/08), "Spring" (5/6/05), and "Easter" (4/15/05). In the 1941 second edition, only four illustrations are in color. *Parrish/Ludwig No. 402*

"Villa Campi" frontispiece from *Italian Villas and Their Gardens. Parrish/ Ludwig No. 345*

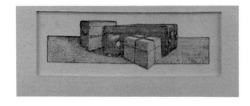

Tailpiece for Lusisti Satis." *Parrish/Ludwig No. 249*

Italian Villas and Their Gardens, by Edith Wharton, with pictures by Maxfield Parrish. Parrish produced fifteen illustrations in color and eleven in black and white for this book. The Century Company, 1904.

"The Reservoir, Villa Falconieri, Frascati" from *Italian Villas and Their Gardens.* *Parrish/Ludwig No. 364*

"The Cascades, Villa Torlonia, Frascati" from *Italian Villas and Their Gardens.* *Parrish/Ludwig No. 365*

"Boboli Garden" from *Italian Villas and Their Gardens.* *Parrish/Ludwig No. 350*

"Gamberaia" from *Italian Villas and Their Gardens.* *Parrish/Ludwig No. 349*

"Villa Corsini, Florence" from *Italian Villas and Their Gardens. Parrish/ Ludwig No. 348*

"Vicobello, Sienna" from *Italian Villas and Their Gardens Parrish/Ludwig No. 354*

"La Palazzina (Villa Gori)" from *Italian Villas and Their Gardens*. Parrish/Ludwig No. 355

"Villa Pia—In the Gardens of the Vatican" from *Italian Villas and Their Gardens*. Parrish/Ludwig No. 358

"Villa D'Este" from *Italian Villas and Their Gardens*. Parrish/Ludwig No. 365

"The Theater at La Palazzina Siena" from *Italian Villas and Their Gardens*. Parrish/Ludwig No. 356

"Villa Medici" from *Italian Villas and Their Gardens*. Parrish/Ludwig No. 359

"Villa Chigi" from *Italian Villas and Their Gardens*. Parrish/Ludwig No. 360

"Pool of Villa D'Este" from *Italian Villas and Their Gardens*. Parrish/Ludwig No. 362

"Villa Lante, Bagnaia" from *Italian Villas and Their Gardens. Parrish/Ludwig No. 366*

"A Garden-niche, Villa Scassi" from *Italian Villas and Their Gardens. Parrish/Ludwig No. 381*

"Villa Isola Bella, Lake Maggiore" from *Italian Villas and Their Gardens. Parrish/Ludwig No. 377*

"Villa Cicogna, Bisuschio" from *Italian Villas and Their Gardens. Parrish/Ludwig No. 376*

"Villa Scassi" from *Italian Villas and Their Gardens. Parrish/Ludwig No. 382*

"In the Gardens of Isola Bella" from *Italian Villas and Their Gardens. Parrish/ Ludwig No. 380*

"Gateway of the Botanic Garden, Padua" from *Italian Villas and Their Gardens. Parrish/Ludwig No. 373*

"View of Val San Zibio, near Battaglia" from *Italian Villas and Their Gardens. Parrish/Ludwig No. 370*

"Villa Pliniana" from *Italian Villas and Their Gardens. Parrish/Ludwig No. 375*

"Val San Zibio, near Battaglia" from *Italian Villas and Their Gardens. Parrish/Ludwig No. 371*

"Villa Valmarana, Vicenza" from *Italian Villas and Their Gardens. Parrish/Ludwig No. 372*

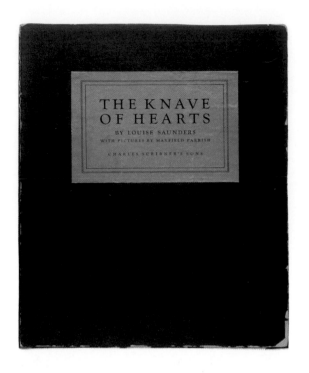

"Romance," cover linings. *Parrish/Ludwig No. 696*

The box that contained the first edition of *Knave of Hearts*

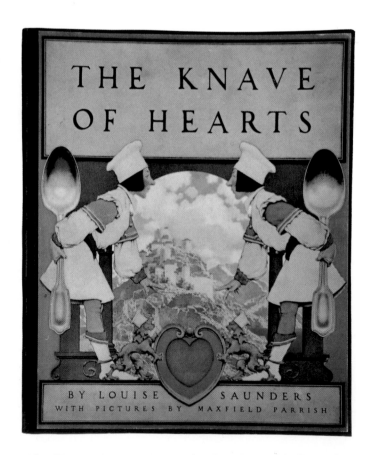

The bookplate in *The Knave of Hearts. Parrish/Ludwig No. 697*

The Knave of Hearts, by Louise Saunders, with illustrations by Maxfield Parrish. Parrish did twenty-three delightful, color illustrations for this book. Charles Scribner's Sons, 1925. *Parrish/Ludwig No. 695*

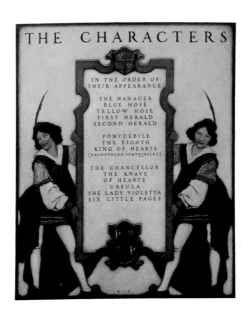

"Lady Violetta about to Make the Tarts,"
frontispiece from *The Knave of Hearts*.
Parrish/Ludwig No. 698

"The Characters" from *The Knave of Hearts*,
page 5. *Parrish/Ludwig No. 691*

"Two Chefs at Table" from *The Knave of
Hearts*, page 9. *Parrish/Ludwig No. 700*

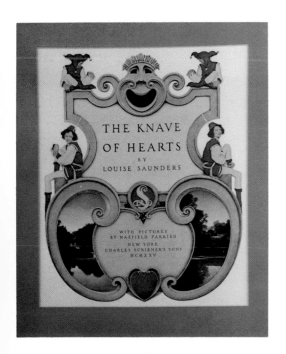

The title page from *The Knave of Hearts*.
Parrish/Ludwig No. 690

"The Manager Draws the Curtain" from
The Knave of Hearts, page 7. *Parrish/
Ludwig No. 699*

"Two Pastry Cooks: Blue Hose and Yellow
Hose" from *The Knave of Hearts*, page 11.
Parrish/Ludwig No. 692

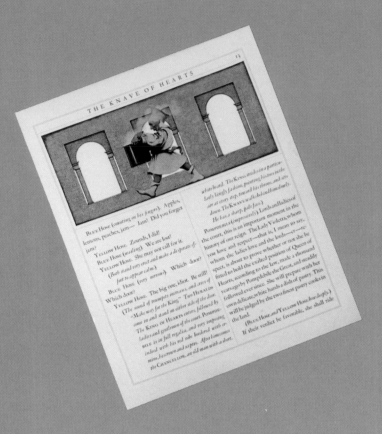

"Chef Carrying Cauldron" from *The Knave of Hearts*, page 13. *Parrish/Ludwig No. 693*

"Chef Between Two Lobsters" from *The Knave of Hearts*, page 17. *Parrish/Ludwig No. 702*

"Entrance of Pompdebile, King of Hearts" from *The Knave of Hearts*, page 15. *Parrish/Ludwig No. 701*

"Lady Ursula Kneeling before Pompdebile, King of Hearts" from *The Knave of Hearts*, page 19. *Parrish/Ludwig No. 703*

"The Youth and the Frog" from *The Knave of Hearts*, page 21. *Parrish/Ludwig No. 704*

"Two Cooks Peeling Potatoes" from *The Knave of Hearts*, page 33. *Parrish/Ludwig No. 708*

"The Gardener Wheeling the Vegetables" from *The Knave of Hearts*, page 29. *Parrish/ Ludwig No. 718*

"The Six Little Ingredients" from *The Knave of Hearts*, page 23. *Parrish/ Ludwig No. 705*

"The King and the Chancellor at the Kitchen Door" from *The Knave of Hearts*, page 31. *Parrish/Ludwig No. 707*

"The Knave" from *The Knave of Hearts*, page 35. *Parrish/Ludwig No. 709*

"Violetta and Knave Examining the Tarts" from *The Knave of Hearts*, page 27. *Parrish/ Ludwig No. 706*

"Fool in Green" from The Knave of Hearts, page 37. *Parrish/Ludwig No. 710*

"The Serenade" from The Knave of Hearts, page 31. *Parrish/Ludwig No. 712*

"The End, The Manager Bows" from The Knave of Hearts, page 47. *Parrish/Ludwig No. 694*

"The King Tastes the Tarts" from *The Knave of Hearts*, page 39. *Parrish/Ludwig No. 711*

"The Knave Watches Violetta Depart" from The Knave of Hearts, page 43. *Parrish/ Ludwig No. 713*

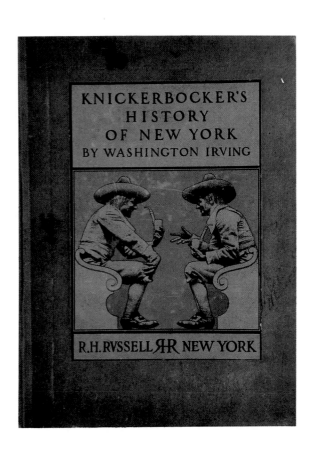

Knickerbocker's History of New York, by Washington Irving. R.H. Russell, New York, 1900. Parrish did the cover and eight black and white illustrations. *Parrish/Ludwig No. 269*

"Indian Drinking Rum," *Knickerbocker's History of New York. Parrish/Ludwig No. 213*

"Oloffe the Dreamer up in the Treetop," *Knickerbocker's History of New York. Parrish/Ludwig No. 181*

"Saint Nicholas," *Knickerbocker's History of New York. Parrish/Ludwig No. 215*

"Vouter Van Twiller," *Knickerbocker's History of New York. Parrish/Ludwig No. 187*

"The Witch," *Knickerbocker's History of New York. Parrish/Ludwig No. 235*

"Peter on the Roof," *Knickerbocker's History of New York. Parrish/Ludwig No. 250*

"Blacksmith," *Knickerbocker's History of New York. Parrish/Ludwig No. 234*

"A phalanx of oyster-fed Pavonians...who had remained behind to digest the enormous dinner they had eaten," *Knickerbocker's History of New York. Parrish/Ludwig No. 251*

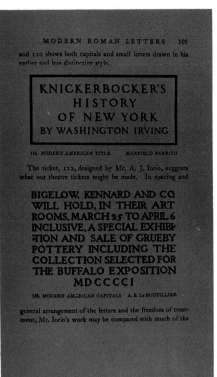

Title page for *Mother Goose in Prose*.
Parrish/Ludwig No. 135

"Pictures by Maxfield Parrish," from *Mother
Goose in Prose*. *Parrish/Ludwig No. 123*

Letters & Lettering: A Treatise with 200 Examples, Bates & Guild
Co., Frank C. Brown, 1921, contained these examples of Parrish's
lettering.

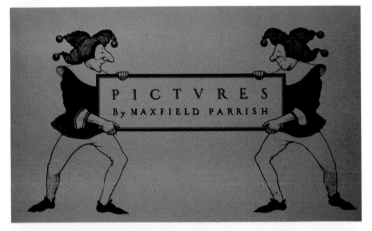

Mother Goose in Prose by L. Frank Baum, Way and Williams
publishers, Chicago, 1897. In addition to the cover, printed in six
colors, Parrish did extensive black and white work for this book.
Parrish/Ludwig No. 122

"There was a little man who had a little gun," frontispiece, *Mother
Goose in Prose*. *Parrish/Ludwig No. 136*

"Little Boy Blue," *Mother Goose in Prose. Parrish/Ludwig No. 166*

"Old King Cole," *Mother Goose in Prose. Parrish/Ludwig No. 165*

"The Black Sheep," *Mother Goose in Prose. Parrish/Ludwig No. 165*

"The Wond'rous Wise Man," *Mother Goose in Prose. Parrish/Ludwig No. 134*

"Jack Horner," *Mother Goose in Prose. Parrish/Ludwig No. 163*

"Little Bo-Peep," *Mother Goose in Prose. Parrish/Ludwig No. 167*

"The Man in the Moon," *Mother Goose in Prose. Parrish/Ludwig No. 144*

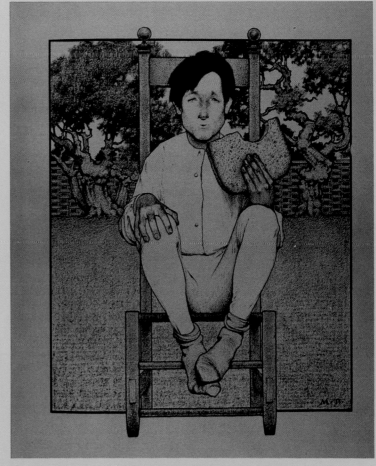

"Tommy Tucker," *Mother Goose in Prose. Parrish/Ludwig No. 142*

"Tom, the Piper's Son," *Mother Goose in Prose. Parrish/Ludwig No. 164*

"Three Wise Men of Gotham," *Mother Goose in Prose. Parrish/Ludwig No. 162*

"Humpty, Dumpty," *Mother Goose in Prose. Parrish/Ludwig No. 158*

Peterkin, Gabrielle E. Jackson, published by Duffield and Company with this cover by Parrish, 1912. *Parrish/Ludwig No. 573*

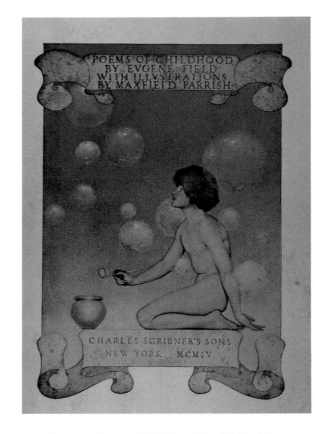

Poems of Childhood by Eugene Field, with illustrations by Maxfield Parrish. Charles Scribner's Sons, 1904. The volume contained nine color illustrations plus the lining papers. Parrish/Ludwig No. 367

Title page, *Poems of Childhood. Parrish/Ludwig No. 368*

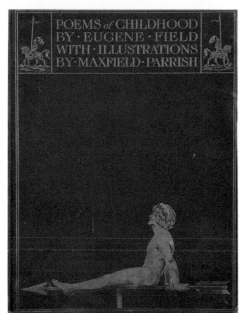

A later edition of *Poems of Childhood Parrish/Ludwig No. 547*

"With Trumpet and Drum," *Poems of Childhood. Parrish/Ludwig No. 343*

Cover lining, *Poems of Childhood. Parrish/Ludwig No. 369*

The Sugar-plum Tree

"The Sugar-Plum Tree," *Poems of Childhood. Parrish/Ludwig No. 552*

THE LITTLE PEACH

The Little Peach

"*The Little Peach," Poems of Childhood. Parrish/Ludwig No. 554*

The Fly-away Horse

"The Fly-Away Horse," *Poems of Childhood. Parrish/Ludwig No. 374*

Wynken, Blynken, and Nod

"Wynken, Blynken, and Nod," *Poems of Childhood. Parrish/Ludwig No. 342*

The Dinkey-bird

"*The Dinkey-Bird," Poems of Childhood. Parrish/Ludwig No. 378*

Shuffle-shoon and Amber-locks

"Shuffle-Shoon and Amber-Locks," *Poems of Childhood. Parrish/ Ludwig No. 379*

"Seein' Things," *Poems of Childhood. Parrish/Ludwig No. 553*

A Wonder Book and Tanglewood Tales by Nathaniel Hawthorne. Illustrated by Maxfield Parrish. Duffield and Company, New York, 1910. The hard cover feature "Circe's Palace." Included in the volume were ten color illustrations plus cover linings. *Parrish/Ludwig No. 448* The dust jacket of *A Wonder Book and Tanglewood Tales* feature "Atlas." *Parrish/Ludwig No. 450*

Tinkering with Tools, Henry H. Saylor, Little, Brown & Company, 1903. This volume contained two photographs of Parrish's workshop.

"Jason and the Talking Oak," *A Wonder Book and Tanglewood Tales. Parrish/ Ludwig No. 452*

"Atlas," *A Wonder Book and Tanglewood Tales. Parrish/Ludwig No. 450*

"The Fountain of Pirene," *A Wonder Book and Tanglewood Tales. Parrish/Ludwig No. 454*

"Pandora," *A Wonder Book and Tangle-wood Tales. Parrish/Ludwig No. 459*

"Bellerophon by the Fountain of Pirene," *A Wonder Book and Tanglewood Tales. Parrish/Ludwig No. 455*

"Cadmus Sowing the Dragon's Teeth," *A Wonder Book and Tanglewood Tales. Parrish/Ludwig No. 449*

"Circe's Palace," *A Wonder Book and Tanglewood Tales. Parrish/Ludwig No. 448*

"Jason and His Teacher," *A Wonder Book and Tanglewood Tales. Parrish/Ludwig No. 456*

Parrish's "Tranquility" brightens the cover of *You and Your Work* by Robert Kemp. It graced the 1936 Brown & Bigelow Calendar as "Peaceful Valley." It is copyrighted to Brown-Robertson Company of New York, and the image is about the same size as the prints they marketed for a brief period. 1948. Overall size 5″ x 8½″.

"Proserpina," *A Wonder Book and Tanglewood Tales. Parrish/Ludwig No. 458*

"The Argonauts in Quest of the Golden Fleece," *A Wonder Book and Tanglewood Tales. Parrish/Ludwig No. 457*

Magazine Illustrations

According to Ludwig, Parrish's start in magazine illustration began by chance. Thomas W. Ball, of Harper and Brother's Art Department, was visiting an exhibit at the Pennsylvania Academy of Fine Arts, where studies for Parrish's Mask and Wig Club decorations were being displayed. He invited Parrish to submit a cover design for the Easter, 1895 issue of *Harper's Bazar*. Parrish submitted two designs, one which was used for that issue and one which was used for the Easter cover of *Harper's Young People*.

It was the beginning of a long and fruitful aspect of Parrish's career, though one about which he had mixed emotions. Parrish's imaginative covers and illustrations have adorned a variety of magazines, including, most notably, *Harper's, Scribner's, Collier's, Life,* and *Century*.

American Agriculturist

Cover for the *American Agriculturist,* January 1, 1897. *Parrish/Ludwig No. 076*

Book Buyer, Christmas, 1898. *Parrish/Ludwig No. 183*

American Magazine

"Twilight" and a valentine Parrish created for his eighteen year-old daughter appeared with this article in *American Magazine*, May, 1930. The article reviews Parrish's career briefly and suggests that at that time "Daybreak" hung in over 200,000 homes, and "'Maxfield Parrish blue' is now...one of the most widely admired colors produced by any modern artist." *Parrish/Ludwig No. 731 & 732*

Book Buyer

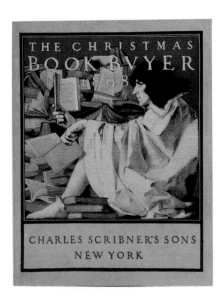

Book Buyer cover, April, 1899. *Parrish/Ludwig No. 207*

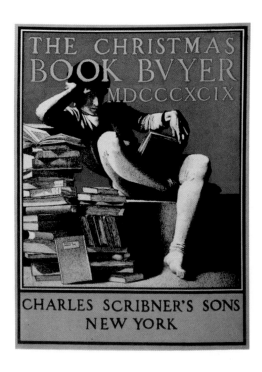

Book Buyer, Christmas, 1899. *Parrish/Ludwig No. 219*

Book News

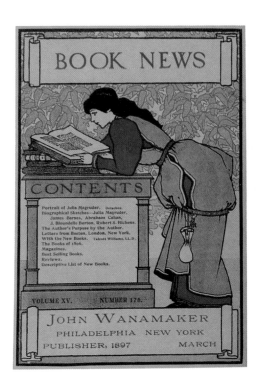

Book News, October, 1895. *Parrish/Ludwig No. 020*

Book News, June, 1897. *Parrish/Ludwig No. 097*

Book News, March, 1897. This was a standard cover with its first use in March, 1896. There was some variation in color. *Parrish/Ludwig No. 049*

The Century

Illustrations "Christmas Eve," a poem by Ednah Proctor Clarke, *Century Magazine,* December, 1898. This is "Shepherds with Sheep." *Parrish/Ludwig No. 204*

"Madonna and Child" frontispiece from Ednah Proctor Clarke's "Christmas Eve." *Parrish/Ludwig No. 205*

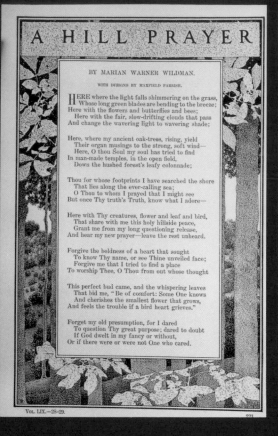

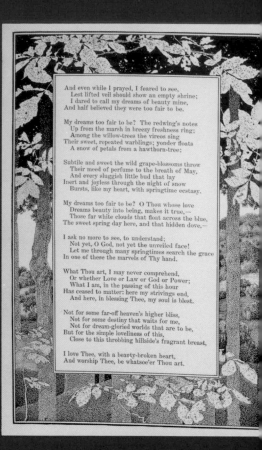

Page decorations and illustration for Marian Warner Wildman's poem "A Hill Prayer," *Century Magazine*, December, 1899. *Parrish/Ludwig No. 254, 255, & 256*

Illustration for "The Story of Ann Powell," *Century Magazine*, July, 1900. *Parrish/Ludwig No. 257*

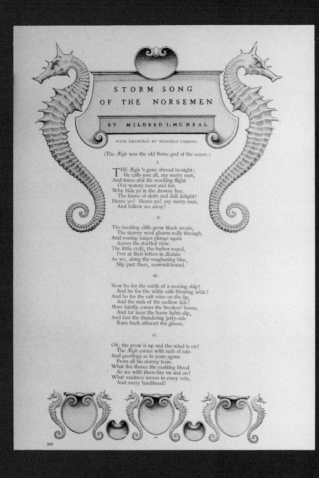

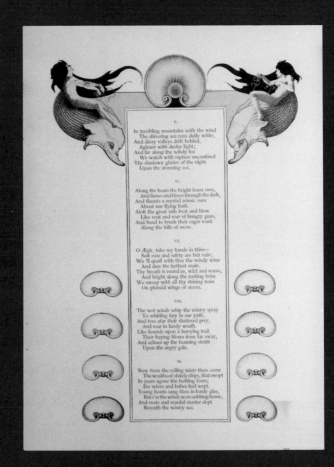

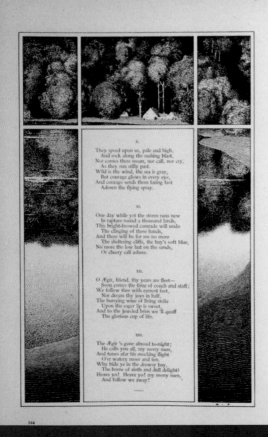

**Page decorations and an illustration for Mildred I. McNeal's
"Storm Song of the Norsemen,"** *Century Magazine*, **January, 1901.**
Parrish/Ludwig No. 260, 261, 262, and 259

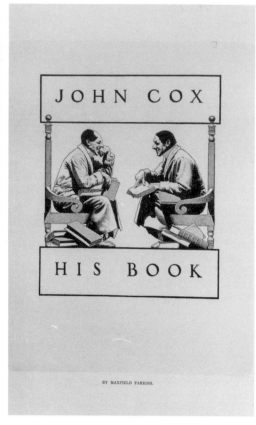

"Milkmaid," illustration for John Milton's "L'Allegro," *Century Magazine*, December, 1901. *Parrish/Ludwig No. 293*

"Such sights as youthful poets dream on summer eves by haunted streams," illustration for John Milton's "L'allegro," *Century Magazine*, December, 1901. *Parrish/Ludwig No. 291*

Illustration from "The Appeal of the Bookplate," *Century Magazine*, December, 1901. John Cox is a fictitious name. *Parrish/Ludwig No. 296*

"Straight mine eyes hath caught new pleasures," illustration for "L'Allegro." *Parrish/Ludwig No. 292*

"Stream running through grazing land," (Ludwig) from "The Great Southwest," Part I, *Century Magazine,* May, 1902. *Parrish/Ludwig No. 317*

"The Mexican," *Century Magazine,* May, 1902. *Parrish/Ludwig No. 321*

"Desert landscape with blue mountain" (Ludwig), Century Magazine, May, 1902.

"Cow-Boys," *Century Magazine,* May, 1902. *Parrish/Ludwig No. 320*

"The bed of a typical Southwest river—A raging torrent perhaps for a month, but dry as dust for the other eleven months," illustration for "The Great Southwest," Part II, "The Desert," *Century Magazine,* June, 1902. *Parrish/Ludwig No. 323*

"A gold-mine in the desert," illustration, *Century,* June, 1902. *Parrish/Ludwig No. 324*

"Sunrise in the Desert," illustration, *Century*, June, 1902. *Parrish/ Ludwig No. 325*

"Irrigating-canal in the Salt River Valley," illustration, "The Great Southwest," Part III, "Irrigation," *Century Magazine,* July, 1902. *Parrish/Ludwig No. 328*

"The Cactus Came, Especially the Prickly-Pear," illustration, *Century,* August, 1902. *Parrish/Ludwig No. 333*

"Night in the Desert," illustration, *Century*, June, 1902. *Parrish/ Ludwig No. 326*

"The Sign of a Thirsty Land," illustration, "The Great Southwest," Part IV, "The Tragedy of the Range," *Century Magazine,* August, 1902. *Parrish/Ludwig No. 332*

"In the Track of the Flood," illustration, *Century,* August, 1902. *Parrish/Ludwig No. 334*

"The Grand Canyon of the Colorado," illustration, "Seven Illustrations for 'The Great Southwest.'" This illustration and those that followed first appeared in black and white. Here, in the November, 1902 issue of *Century Magazine,* they were presented in color. This image first appeared in Part I, May, 1902. *Parrish/Ludwig No. 320*

"The Desert without Water," first appeared in Part III, July, 1902. *Parrish/ Ludwig No. 329*

"Formal Growth in the Desert," first appeared in Part II, June, 1902. *Parrish/ Ludwig No. 327*

"Pueblo Dwellings," first appeared in Part I, May, 1902. *Parrish/Ludwig No. 322*

"The Desert with Water," first appeared in Part III, July, 1902. *Parrish/Ludwig No. 330*

"Water Let in on a Field of Alfalfa," from Part III, July, 1902. *Parrish/Ludwig No. 331*

"Bill Sachs: The Flying Dutchman; An often held up stage-driver of the old days," from Part IV, August, 1902. *Parrish/Ludwig No. 335*

"Italian Villas and Their Gardens" appeared first in *Century Magazine* as an ongoing series, beginning November, 1903 and continuing through October, 1904. All of the images were gathered together in book form and published by The Century Company in November, 1904. Following are some of the images as they appeared in the magazine. This is the title page from November, 1903. *Parrish/Ludwig No. 344*

"Villa Campi," frontispiece from the November, 1903 issue of *Century. Parrish/ Ludwig No. 345*

"Villa Gori," *Century Magazine,* December, 1903. *Parrish/Ludwig No. 348*

"Villa Corsini," *Century,* November, 1903. *Parrish/Ludwig No. 348*

"The Dome of St. Peter's, from the Vatican Gardens," *Century,* February, 1904. *Parrish/Ludwig No. 357*

"Villa d'Este," *Century*, February, 1904.
Parrish/Ludwig No. 359

"The Pool of the Villa d'Este," *Century,*
February, 1904. *Parrish/Ludwig
No. 362*

"View at Val San Zibio," *Century*, October,
1904. *Parrish/Ludwig No. 370*

"Torlonia (formerly Villa Conte)", *Century,*
February, 1904. *Parrish/Ludwig
No. 363*

"Val San Zibio," *Century*, October, 1904.
Parrish/Ludwig No. 371

"Gateway of the Botanic Gardens of Padua,"
Century, October, 1904. *Parrish/Ludwig
No. 373*

"Ode to Autumn." *Century Magazine*, November, 1904. Two page illustration of John Keats "Ode to Autumn." *Parrish/Ludwig No. 385*

A JOURNEY THROUGH SUNNY PROVENCE IN THE DAYS OF KING RENÉ

"A Journey Through Sunny Provence in the Days of King Rene?" *Century Magazine, March, 1905. This image was originally used in St. Nicholas Magazine* in December, 1898, with the caption "The Page of Count Reynaurd." *Parrish/Ludwig No. 176*

"I Am Sick of Being a Princess." An illustration for Kate Whiting Patch's "The Princess and the Boy," *Century Magazine*, December, 1904. *Parrish/Ludwig No. 388*

"The Sandman," *Century Magazine*, March, 1905. According to Ludwig the painting this is based on was a copy of the original redone at the owners' request to make it lighter. The original was done in 1896 *Parrish/Ludwig No. 070*. This was done in 1902-1903. The original was seen by Parrish as the most important of his early career (Ludwig, page 17). *Parrish/Ludwig No. 346*

"A Master of Make Believe," an early biographical sketch of Maxfield Parrish by Christian Brinton, included ten illustrations of his work. This is the title page for the *Whist Reference Book,* 1898. *Century Magazine,* July, 1912. *Parrish/Ludwig No. 173*

An illustration for Florence Wilkinson's "Seven Green Pools at Cintra," *Century Magazine,* August, 1910. Ludwig reports that the background of the original painting was later painted out and the work renamed "Griselda." *Parrish/Ludwig No. 518*

"Be Good—Ellen—Her Book" bookplate for Ellen Biddle Shipman. *Century Magazine,* July, 1912. *Parrish/Ludwig No. 506*

"Pierrot: A Paper Cut-Out by Maxfield Parrish," *Century Magazine,* July, 1912. Parrish used cut-outs like this to design his greater works. This Pierrot may be found sitting on the steps in "A Florentine Fete," one of the murals at the Curtis Publishing Company. *Parrish/Ludwig No. 624*

"Proving It by the Book," *Century Magazine,* April, 1911. *Parrish/Ludwig No. 499*

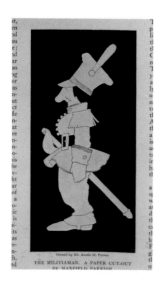

"Humpty Dumpty" from *Mother Goose in Prose, Century Magazine,* July, 1912. *Parrish/Ludwig No. 158*

"'Shabby Genteel': A Paper Cut-out by Maxfield Parrish," *Century Magazine,* July 4, 1908. *Parrish/Ludwig No. not assigned*

"Two Girlish Figures: A Paper Cut-out by Maxfield Parrish." These are studies for (left) "Love's Pilgrimage," *Parrish/Ludwig No. 590,* and (right) "Lazy Land," *Parrish/Ludwig No. 589,* from "The Florentine Fete."

Top: "Profile of Girl's Head: A Paper Cut-out by Maxfield Parrish." *Parrish/Ludwig No. not assigned* Bottom: "Design for the Outside of an Envelope." *Century Magazine*, July, 1912.*Parrish/Ludwig No. 515*

"The Militiaman: A Paper Cut-out by Maxfield," *Century Magazine,* July, 1912. The finished work appeared on the cover of *Collier's,* July 4, 1908. Variation of *Parrish/Ludwig No. 469*

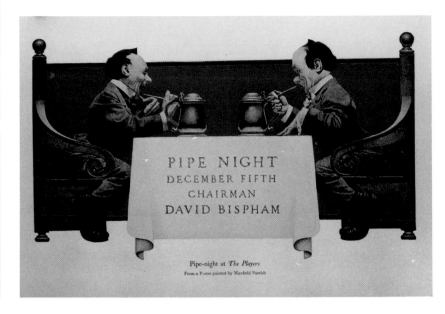

Top: "Old King Cole: Drawn by Maxfield Parrish," from the Mask and Wig Club, Philadelphia, *Parrish/Ludwig No. 027*; Bottom: "A French Cook, On a Fanciful Menu." *Century Magazine*, July, 1912. *Parrish/Ludwig No. 517*

"Pipe Night at *The Players*," *Century Magazine*, December, 1915. *Parrish/Ludwig No. 619*

"Decoration on the Outside of an Envelope Sent by Mail," *Century Magazine*, July, 1912. *Parrish/Ludwig No. 516*

Collier's

Collier's cover, December 3, 1904. *Parrish/Ludwig No. 392*

Century cover, August, 1917. Originally painted as the 1897 *Century* Midsummer Holiday Poster. *Parrish/Ludwig No. 052*

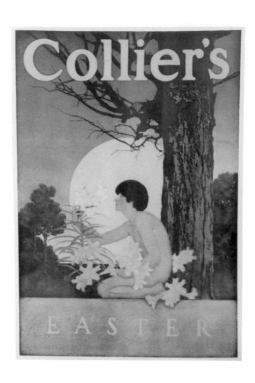

Collier's cover, January 7, 1905. *Parrish/Ludwig No. 395*

Collier's, "Easter" cover, April 15, 1905. *Parrish/Ludwig No. 400*

Collier's cover, "Independence Number," July 1, 1905. *Parrish/Ludwig No. 401*

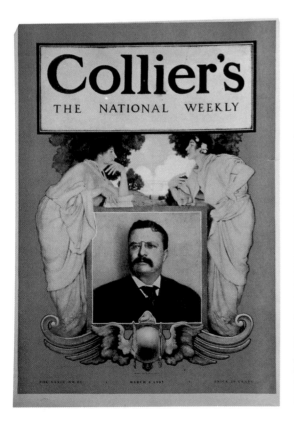

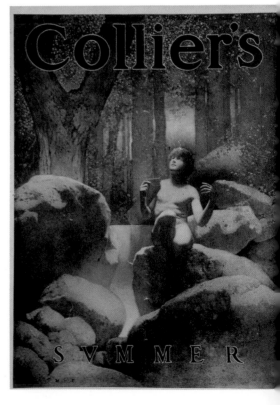

A permanent *Collier's* cover, this is from March 4, 1905 and features Theodore Roosevelt. *Parrish/Ludwig No. 397*

Collier's cover, "Spring," May 6, 1905. *Parrish/Ludwig No. 402*

Collier's cover, "Summer," July 22, 1905. *Parrish/Ludwig No. 404*

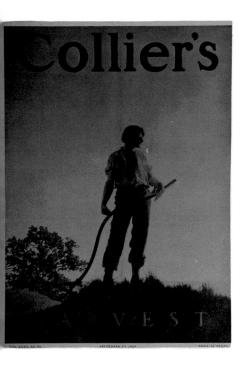

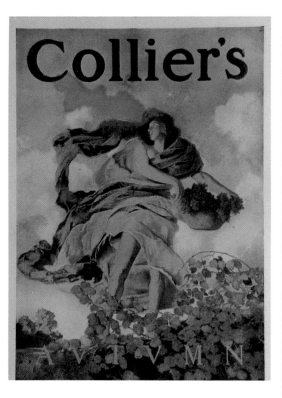

Collier's cover, "Harvest," September 23, 1905. *Parrish/Ludwig No. 405*

Collier's cover, "Autumn," October 28, 1905. *Parrish/Ludwig No. 409*

Collier's cover, "Christmas Number," December 16, 1905. *Parrish/Ludwig No. 406*

Collier's cover, "Out of Doors Number," October 14, 1905. *Parrish/ Ludwig No. 407*

Collier's cover, "Thanksgiving Number," November 18, 1905. *Parrish/Ludwig No. 408*

Collier's cover, "New Year's Number," January 6, 1906. *Parrish/Ludwig No. 422*

Collier's cover, "Lincoln's Birthday Number," February 10, 1906. *Parrish/Ludwig No. 423*

"The History of the Fisherman and the Genie," *Collier's*, April 7, 1906. *Parrish/Ludwig No. 412*

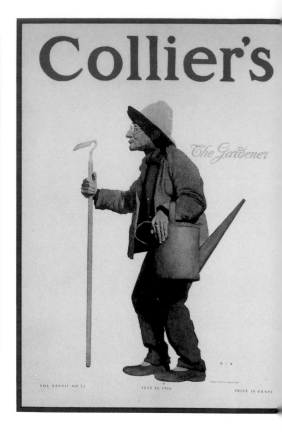

"The Gardener," *Collier's* cover, June 23, 1906. *Parrish/Ludwig No. 426*

Collier's cover, later called "Winter," March 10, 1906. *Parrish/Ludwig No. 424*

Collier's cover, later called "Dawn," May 19, 1906. *Parrish/Ludwig No. 425*

Collier's cover, "Independence Number," July 7, 1906. *Parrish/ Ludwig No. 432*

Collier's cover, later called "The Swing," July 21, 1906. *Parrish/Ludwig No. 430*

Frontispiece for "Prince Agib: The Story of the King's Son," *Collier's*, October 13, 1906. *Parrish/Ludwig No. 411*

Collier's cover, "Thanksgiving," November 17, 1906. *Parrish/Ludwig No. 439*

"The History of Prince Codadad and His Brothers and the Princess of Deryabar," *Collier's*, September 1, 1906. *Parrish/Ludwig No. 419*

"Cassim in the Cave of the Forty Thieves," *Collier's*, November 3, 1906. *Parrish/Ludwig No. 413*

"The Search for the Singing Tree," *Collier's*, December 1, 1906. *Parrish/Ludwig No. 415*

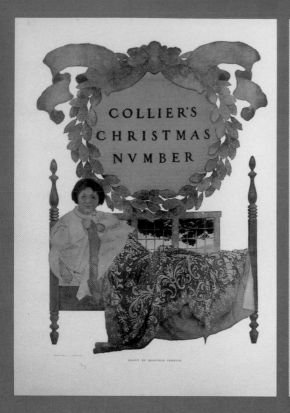

Frontispiece for *Collier's* Christmas Number, December 15, 1906. *Parrish/Ludwig No. 440*

"The City of Brass," *Collier's,* March 16, 1907. *Parrish/Ludwig No. 417*

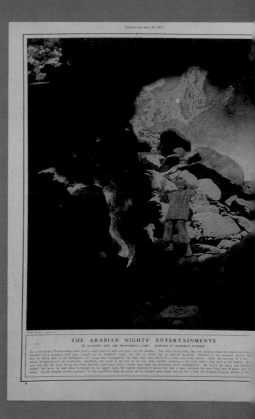

"Aladdin and the Wonderful Lamp," *Collier's*, June 22, 1907. *Parrish/ Ludwig No. 410*

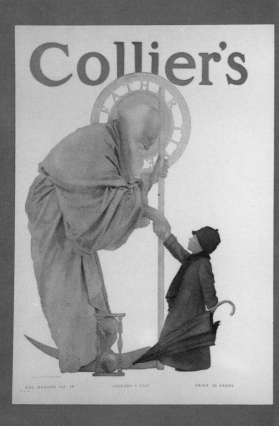

Collier's cover, January 5, 1907. *Parrish/Ludwig No. 442*

"The King of the Black Isles," *Collier's*, May 18, 1907. *Parrish/Ludwig No. 421*

"The Valley of Diamonds," *Collier's,* September 7, 1907. *Parrish/Ludwig No. 416*

"Atlas Holding Up the Sky," May 16, 1908. *Parrish/Ludwig No. 450*

Collier's cover, "Vaudeville" number, June 6, 1908. *Parrish/Ludwig No. 445*

"Oklahoma Comes In," *Collier's* cover, November 30, 1907. *Parrish/Ludwig No. 438*

Headpiece and illustration from *Collier's*, January 11, 1908. The piece at the bottom was on the outside of the package that Parrish used to send his work to *Collier's*. The item announces the forthcoming use of his "Funnygraphs" in future issues of the magazine. *Parrish/Ludwig No. 468*

Collier's cover, July 4, 1908. *Parrish/Ludwig No. 469*

A page heading for the July 4, 1908 issue of *Collier's. Parrish/Ludwig No. not assigned*

"Pierrot," *Collier's* cover, August 8, 1908. *Parrish/Ludwig No. 461*

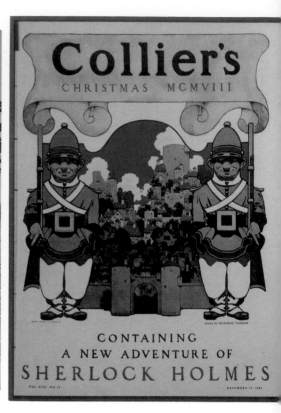

Collier's cover, Christmas number, "Toyland," December 12, 1908. *Parrish/ Ludwig No. 479*

"The Botanist," *Collier's* cover, July 18, 1908. *Parrish/Ludwig No. 471*

Collier's cover, "School Days (Alphabet)," September 12, 1908. *Parrish/Ludwig No. 467*

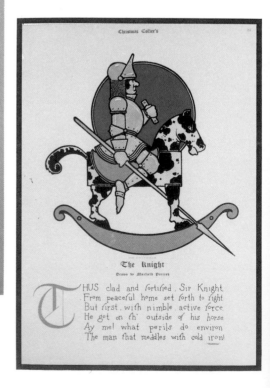

"The Knight," *Collier's*, December 12, 1908. *Parrish/Ludwig No. 484*

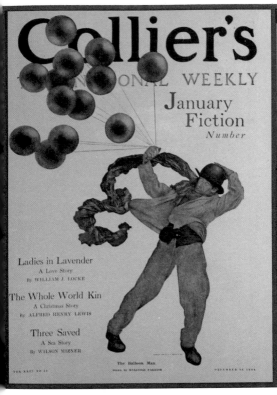

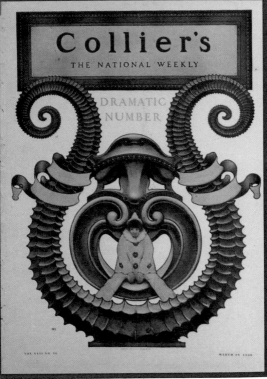

"The Balloon Man" *Collier's* cover, December 26, 1908. *Parrish/Ludwig No. 460*

Collier's "Dramatic Number" cover, "Mask and Pierrot," March 20, 1909. *Parrish/Ludwig No. 487*

"The Lone Fisherman," *Collier's* cover, April 17, 1909. *Parrish/Ludwig No. 493*

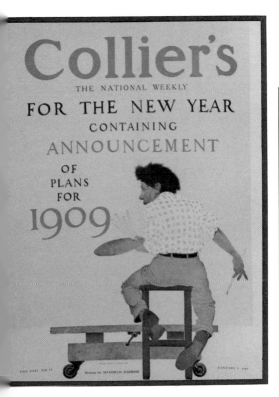

"The Artist" *Collier's* cover, January 2, 1909. *Parrish/Ludwig No. 477*

"April Showers," *Collier's* cover, April 3, 1909. *Parrish/Ludwig No. 573*

Collier's cover, April 24, 1909, with the center section of the "Old King Cole" triptych. *Parrish/Ludwig No. 446*

"The Artist," *Collier's* cover, May 1, 1909.
Parrish/Ludwig No. 475

Collier's cover, "Fiction Number," later called
"The Pirate," June 26, 1909. *Parrish/Ludwig No.
481*

"The Tourist,", *Collier's* cover, July
10, 1909. *Parrish/Ludwig No. 509*

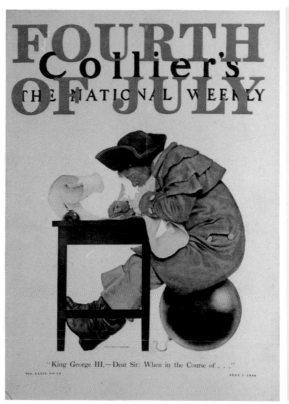

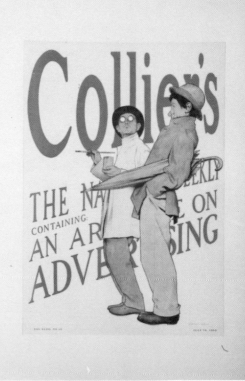

Collier's cover, May 29, 1909, with the right
of the "Old King Cole" triptych. *Parrish/
Ludwig No. 447*

"Fourth of July" Number, *Collier's* cover, July 3,
1909. Originally entitled "Young America Writing
the Declaration of Independence." *Parrish/Ludwig
No. 498*

Collier's cover, "The Signpainter,"
July 24, 1909, "containing an article
on advertising." *Parrish/Ludwig No.
486*

"Pandora: The Paradise of Children,"
Collier's, October 16, 1909. *Parrish/Ludwig
No. 459*

Collier's cover, "Christmas Number,"
December 11, 1909. *Parrish/Ludwig No.
495*

Collier's cover, July 30, 1910. *Parrish/
Ludwig No. 478*

"Thanksgiving Number," *Collier's* cover,
November 20, 1909. *Parrish/Ludwig No.
507*

"Outdoors America" Number, *Collier's*
cover, January 8, 1910. *Parrish/Ludwig
No. 496*

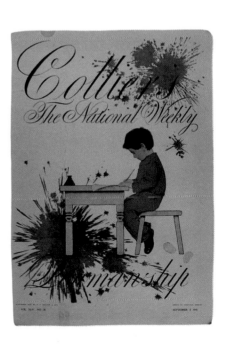

"Penmanship," *Collier's* cover, September
3, 1910. *Parrish/Ludwig No. 491*

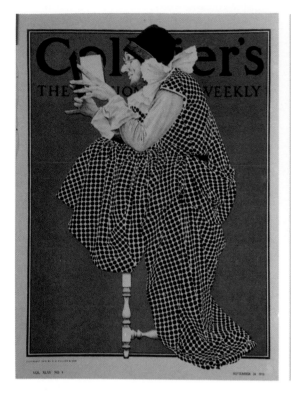

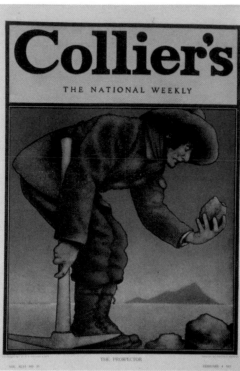

Collier's cover, "The Idiot" or "The Book Lover," September 24, 1910. *Parrish/Ludwig No. 583*

"The Prospector," *Collier's* cover, February 4, 1911. *Parrish/Ludwig No. 494*

Collier's cover, sometimes called "Man with Green Apple" or "Nature Lover," April 1, 1911. *Parrish/Ludwig No. 584*

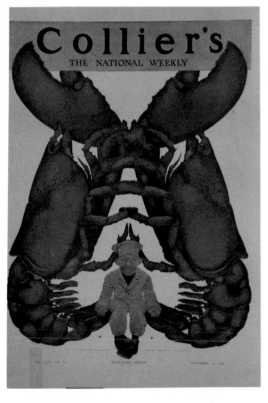

Collier's cover, November 26, 1910. *Parrish/Ludwig No. 476*

Collier's cover, "Comic Scottish Soldier," March 11, 1911. *Parrish/Ludwig No. 490*

"April," *Collier's*, April 8, 1911. *Parrish/Ludwig No. 489*

"Arithmetic," *Collier's* cover, September 30, 1911. *Parrish/ Ludwig No. 492*

Collier's cover, November 16, 1912. *Parrish/ Ludwig No. 480*

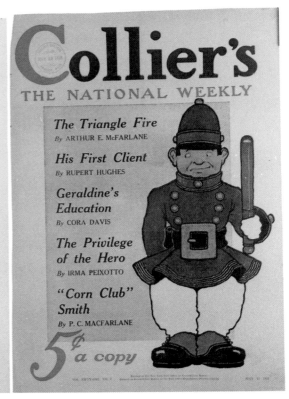

Collier's cover, May 17, 1913. *Parrish/Ludwig No. 468*

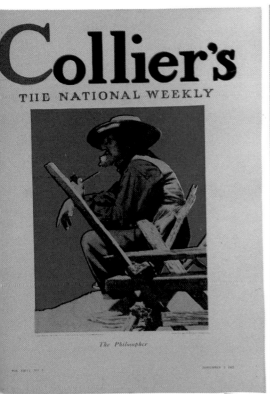

"The Philosopher," *Collier's* cover, November 2, 1912. *Parrish/ Ludwig No. 508*

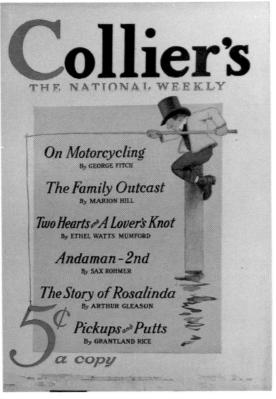

Collier's cover, May 10, 1913. *Parrish/Ludwig No. 462*

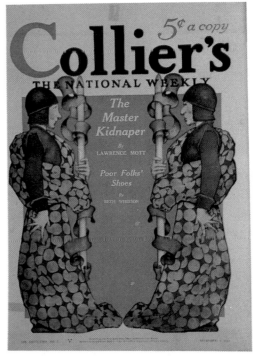

Collier's cover, November 1, 1913. *Parrish/ Ludwig No. 488*

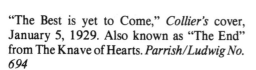

"The Best is yet to Come," *Collier's* cover, January 5, 1929. Also known as "The End" from The Knave of Hearts. *Parrish/Ludwig No. 694*

Collier's cover, July 20, 1929. *Parrish/Ludwig No. 701*

"Jack Frost," *Collier's* cover, October 24, 1936. *Parrish/Ludwig No. 761*

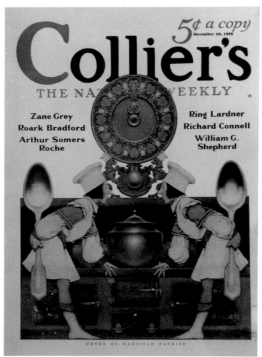

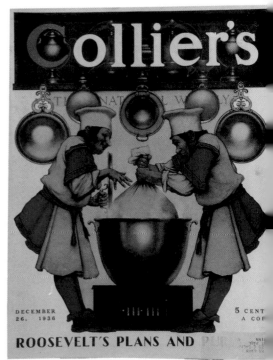

Collier's cover, May 11, 1929. "The Knave Watches Violetta Depart *Parrish/Ludwig No. 713*

Collier's cover, November 30, 1929. From *The Knave of Hearts. Parrish/Ludwig No. 692*

Collier's cover, December 26, 1936. *Parrish/Ludwig No. 764*

The Critic

An illustration of Parrish's prize winning design for a Columbia Bicycle poster in *The Critic*, April 4, 1896. This is one of 525 entries in a contest and exhibition in New York, sponsored by the Pope Manufacturing Co. According to the article the illustration first appeared in a New York *Tribune* news story.

Everybody's Magazine

An illustration for "The Temptation of Ezekial", *Everybody's Magazine*, December, 1901. *Parrish/Ludwig No. 316*

Harper's Bazar

Harper's Bazar, Easter, 1895. This was Parrish's first work for Harper Brothers. *Parrish/Ludwig No. 019*

"Cinderella," *Harper's Bazaar* cover, March, 1914. Ludwig reports that this was originally designed for the cover of *Hearst's* magazine, but was used instead on this Hearst publication. *Parrish/Ludwig No. 600*

Harper's Monthly

Parrish designed the border around this photograph of African Buffalo in *Harper's New Monthly Magazine*, April, 1898. *Parrish/Ludwig No. 171*

Harper's Monthly Magazine, Christmas, 1900. Permanent cover design. *Parrish/Ludwig No. 278*

Harper's Monthly Magazine, June, 1901. Color variation in permanent cover design. *Parrish/Ludwig No. 278*

Harper's Round Table

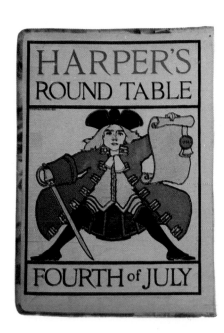

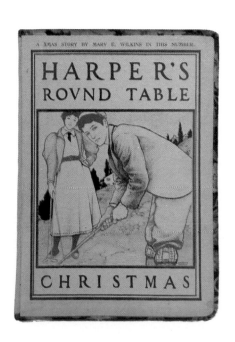

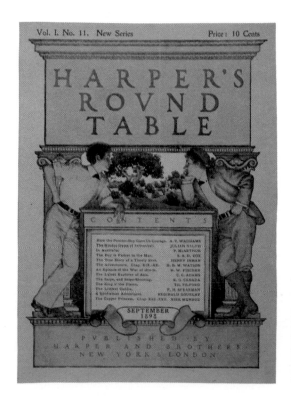

Harper's Round Table, "Fourth of July" number, 1895. *Parrish/Ludwig No. 031*

Harper's Round Table, Christmas issue, 1896. *Parrish/Ludwig No. 075*

Harper's Round Table, September, 1898, permanent cover. *Parrish/Ludwig No. 120*

Harper's Weekly

Harper's Weekly cover, "Bicycle Number," April 11, 1896. Front cover. *Parrish/Ludwig No. 039*

The "Christmas" number cover, *Harper's Weekly,* December 19, 1896. *Parrish/Ludwig No. 062*

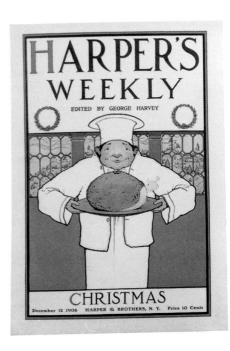

Harper's Weekly, Christmas number, December 12, 1908. The image on this cover is the same as that used on the December 14, 1895 Christmas cover. *Parrish/Ludwig No. 033*

The back cover of the April 11, 1896 issue of *Harper's Weekly* carried this companion piece by Parrish advertising Columbia Bicycles. *Parrish/Ludwig No. 045*

Harper's Weekly cover, Christmas, December 18, 1897. *Parrish/Ludwig No. 112*

"His Christmas Dinner," an illustration for *Harper's Weekly,* December 8, 1900. *Parrish/Ludwig No. 303*

Harper's Young People

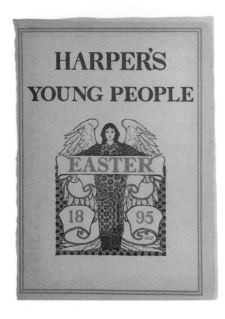

Harper's Young People, Easter, 1895. This angelic illustration was Parrish's first national cover. *Parrish/Ludwig No. 023*

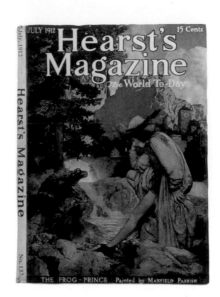

"The Frog Prince." *Hearst's Magazine* cover, July, 1912. *Parrish/Ludwig No. 595*

"Hermes." *Hearst's Magazine* cover, September, 1912. *Parrish/Ludwig No. 597*

Hearst's Magazine

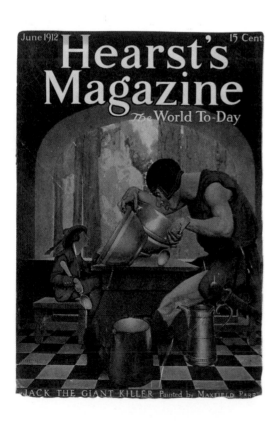

"Jack the Giant Killer." *Hearst's Magazine* cover, June, 1912. *Parrish/Ludwig No. 594*

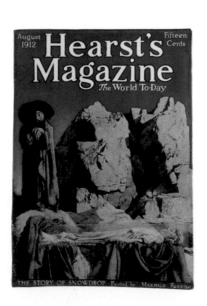

"The Story of Snow Drop." *Hearst's Magazine* cover, August, 1912. *Parrish/Ludwig No. 596*

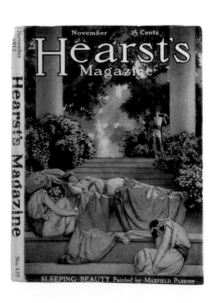

"Sleeping Beauty." *Hearst's Magazine* cover, November, 1912. *Parrish/Ludwig No. 598*

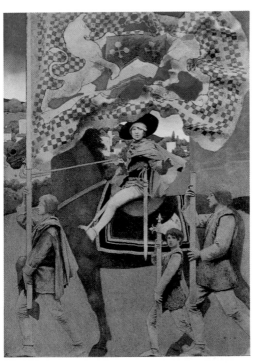

"Puss In Boots." *Hearst's Magazine* cover, May, 1914. *Parrish/Ludwig No. 599*

"Every plunge of our bows brought us nearer to the Happy Island," *The Illustrated London News*, December, 1913. *Parrish/Ludwig No. 548*

"Dies Irae" color illustration from *International Studio*, July, 1906. *Parrish/Ludwig No. 545*

The Illustrated London News

The Ladies' Home Journal

"Everyboy Interviews the Benign Dragon that Fought St. George," *The Illustrated London News*, December, 1910. Also known as "The Reluctant Dragon." *Parrish/Ludwig No. 549*

"At the Passing of the Toys, The Friendly Man in the Moon," also known as "A Departure," *The Illustrated London News*, December 1922. *Parrish/Ludwig No. 551*

The Ladies' Home Journal cover, June, 1896. *Parrish/Ludwig No. 050*

The Ladies' Home Journal cover, June, 1901. *Parrish/Ludwig No. 282*

"Air Castles." *The Ladies' Home Journal* cover, September, 1904. Parrish won a $1000 prize for this image in a *Ladies' Home Journal* cover design competition. *Parrish/Ludwig No. 557*

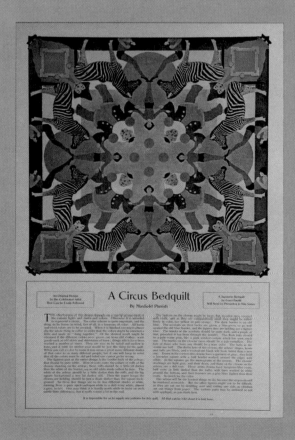

"The Little Peach," illustrated Eugene Field's poem in the March, 1903 issue of *Ladies' Home Journal*. It later graced the pages of *Poems of Childhood. Parrish/Ludwig No. 554*

"A Circus Bedspread." One of a series of Bedspread designs by popular artists, this appeared in the *Ladies' Home Journal* in March, 1905. *Parrish/Ludwig No. 561*

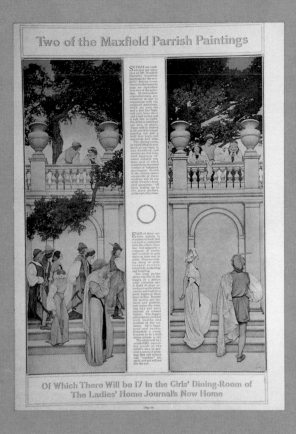

"Two Maxfield Parrish Paintings," *Ladies' Home Journal, May, 1912. "Love's Pilgrimage," Parrish/Ludwig No. 590,* and "Lazy Land," *Parrish/Ludwig No. 589,* from "The Florentine Fete."

"Christmas, 1912" cover, *The Ladies' Home Journal.* "Call to Joy" from the Curtis Publishing murals. *Parrish/Ludwig No. 592*

"Showers of Fragrance" detail from the murals in the girls' dining room at Curtis Publishing. *The Ladies' Home Journal* cover, July, 1912. *Parrish/Ludwig No. 588*

The Ladies' Home Journal, May, 1913. From the Florentine Fete murals, "Buds Below the Roses." *Parrish/Ludwig No. 605*

The Ladies' Home Journal cover, June, 1914. "Garden of Opportunity" detail. *Parrish/Ludwig No. 611*

"Sweet Nothings." *The Ladies' Home Journal cover, April, 1921. Parrish/Ludwig No. 610*

"White Birches," *The Ladies' Home Journal*, March, 1930. *Parrish/Ludwig No. 734*

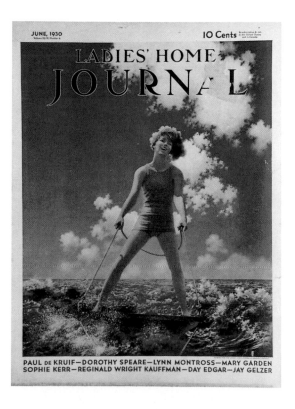

"A Florentine Fete," *The Ladies' Home Journal*, December, 1920. *Parrish/Ludwig No. 624*

"Girl on Surf-board." *The Ladies' Home Journal* cover, June, 1930. *Parrish/Ludwig No. 730*

"Arizona," *The Ladies' Home Journal*, October, 1930. *Parrish/Ludwig No. 739*

"Girl Skiing." *The Ladies' Home Journal*, January, 1931. *Parrish/Ludwig No. 736*

Life

Life cover, Christmas number, December 2, 1899. *Parrish/Ludwig No. 247*

Life's Christmas Number cover, December 1, 1900. *Parrish/Ludwig No. 308*

"Saint Patrick." *Life* cover, March 3, 1904. The original painting was exhibited at the St. Louis World's Fair in 1904. *Parrish/Ludwig No. 555*

"A Merry Christmas." *Life* cover, December 2, 1920. *Parrish/Ludwig No. 660*

"St. Valentine." *Life* cover, February 2, 1905. *Parrish/Ludwig No. 383*

"Humpty Dumpty." *Life* cover, Easter number, March 17, 1921. *Parrish/Ludwig No. 661*

"A Swiss Admiral." *Life* cover, June 30, 1921. *Parrish/Ludwig No. 662*

"Evening." *Life* cover, October 13, 1921. *Parrish/Ludwig No. 665*

Life cover, August 25, 1921. *Parrish/Ludwig No. 663*

"Get Together Number." *Life* cover, November 10, 1921. *Parrish/Ludwig No. 669*

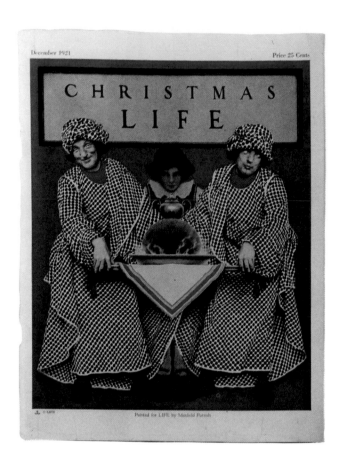

"Christmas *Life*" cover, December, 1921. *Parrish/Ludwig No. 670*

"Morning." *Life* Easter cover, April 6, 1922. *Parrish/Ludwig No. 672*

"A Man of Letters." *Life* cover, January 5, 1922. *Parrish/Ludwig No. 671*

Life "Bookstuff Number" cover, May 11, 1922. Ludwig reports that the original was used as a bulletin board for "The Coffee House." *Parrish/Ludwig No. 673*

Life, June 22, 1922. In a contest to name this image, the winning entry was "He Is a Rogue Indeed Who Robs Life of Its Ends, and Fosters Doubt." Ludwig reports that the original of this image was cut up by the artist, and the head used in a coffee advertisement. Parrish/Ludwig No. 674

"Her Window." Life cover, August 24, 1922. Parrish/Ludwig No. 676

"Tea? Guess Again." Life cover, July 20, 1922. Parrish/Ludwig No. 675

"Masquerade." Life cover, October 29, 1922. Parrish/Ludwig No. 677

"Christmas *Life'* cover, December 7, 1922. *Parrish/Ludwig No. 678*

"The Canyon" graces this Easter cover of *Life*, March 29, 1923. *Parrish/Ludwig No. 685*

"A Dark Futurist." *Life* cover, March 1, 1923. *Parrish/Ludwig No. 684*

Life cover, August 3, 1923. *Parrish/Ludwig No. 687*

"A Good Mixer." *Life* cover, January 31, 1924. *Parrish/Ludwig No. 716*

The Magazine of Light

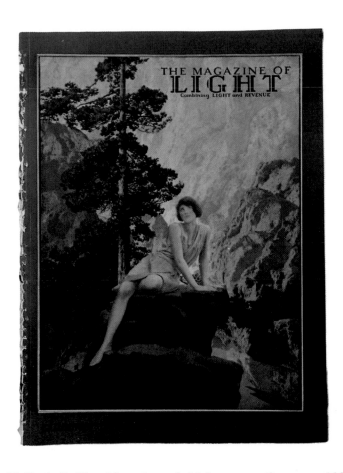

"Solitude." *The Magazine of Light* cover, Summer, 1931. *Parrish/Ludwig No. 740*

McClure's Magazine

"The Waterfall." *The Magazine of Light* cover, February, 1931. *Parrish/Ludwig No. 735*

McClure's Magazine cover, November, 1904. *Parrish/Ludwig No. 384*

McClure's Magazine cover, February, 1905. Permanent cover design. *Parrish/Ludwig No. 394*

The Mentor

"The round-up crew started early the next morning, just about sun-up," illustration from *McClure's*, December, 1904. *Parrish/Ludwig No. 386*

"He swung himself into the saddle and rode away," frontispiece, *McClure's Magazine*, January 1905. *Parrish/Ludwig No. 387*

The Mentor for March, 1922 had an article about the history of the publication of the Arabian Nights, entitled "How the Arabian Nights Came to Us." It had the black and white illustrations from a variety of artists who had treated the subject. Parrish alone is represented in color with *The Fisherman and the Genie"* (*Parrish/Ludwig No. 412*), "The Pirate Ship" (Codadad and his Brothers, *Parrish/Ludwig No. 419*), "Cassim in the Cave of the Forty Thieves" (*Parrish/Ludwig No. 413*), "The King of the Black Isles (*Parrish/Ludwig No. 421*), as small images, and "The City of Brass" (*Parrish/Ludwig No. 417*) as a two-page spread.

Metropolitan Magazine

"Once Upon a Time" illustration for the December, 1904 issue of *Metropolitan Magazine. Parrish/Ludwig No. 384*

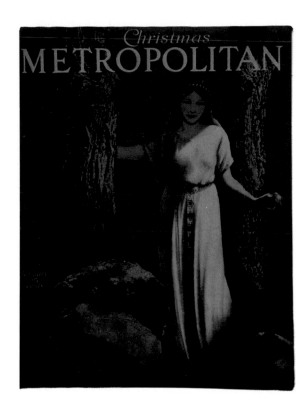

Metropolitan Magazine, Christmas issue, January, 1917. *Parrish/Ludwig No. 601*

Illustration and endpiece for the poem "The Finest Song" by Robert Burns Wilson. Ludwig suggests that these were probably done as one drawing and separated by the publisher. *Metropolitan Magazine, January, 1906. Parrish/Ludwig No. 263*

Minneapolis Tribune-Picture

"Dream Castle in the Sky," owned by the Minneapolis Institute of Arts appeared on the cover of the *Minneapolis Tribune-Picture* for Sunday, August 10, 1975. *Parrish/Ludwig No. 576*

Minnesota Journal of Education

New Hampshire Troubadour

New York Tribune

"The Spirit of Transportation." *Minnesota Journal of Education* cover, October, 1928. *Parrish/Ludwig No. 659*

New Hampshire Troubadour, 1939 World's Fair Edition. Known as "Summer" or "Thy Templed Hills." *Parrish/Ludwig No. 760*

"Pierrot," on the cover of the *New York Tribune* Graphic Section, March 23, 1919 *Parrish/Ludwig No. 461*

New England Homestead

Osteopathic Magazine

New England Homestead, January 2, 1897. The cover is identical to that of the American Agriculturist of the same date. *Parrish/Ludwig No. 076*

"Winter." *New Hampshire Troubadour,* February, 1940. *Parrish/Ludwig No. 769*

"The Spirit of Transportation" on the cover of *Osteopathic Magazine*, July, 1925. *Parrish/Ludwig No. 659*

Outing Magazine

The Red Letter

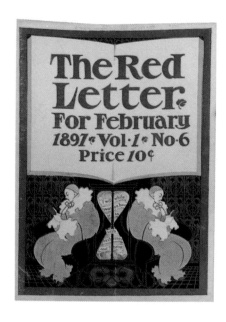

The Outing Magazine permanent cover design, often colored by publisher, September, 1906. *273*

The Outing Magazine cover, April, 1908. Permanent cover design. *Parrish/Ludwig No. 263*

The Red Letter cover, February, 1897. *Parrish/Ludwig No. not assigned*

Progressive Farmer

Progressive Farmer, June, 1952. This image "Sunset on the River" (Thunderheads), was one that Brown & Bigelow did not want for use on their calendars. *Parrish/Ludwig No. 788*

An illustrated article about Maxfield Parrish entitled "A Clever Master of the Grotesque," by Harry D. Hunt *The Red Letter*, 1897. *Parrish/Ludwig No. not assigned*

A design for a silver lamp from "A Clever Master of the Grotesque" *The Red Letter*, 1897. The article identifies it as being for the yacht Merlin. It is assumed that this is the design Ludwig cites as being done for Mr. and Mrs. Cameron Forbes of Massachusetts. *Parrish/Ludwig No. 851*

St. Nicholas

"The Page of Count Reynaurd," illustration from *St. Nicholas Magazine*, December, 1898. *Parrish/Ludwig No. 176*

Illustration from "Molly's Sketch Book—and Mine," an article about collecting autographs. *St. Nicholas Magazine*, December, 1914. *Parrish/Ludwig No. 614*

Saturday Evening Post

The December, 1974 issue of *The Saturday Evening Post* contained this article "The Outer Space Beauty of Maxfield Parrish," by Julie Eisenhower. It included illustrations of Dinkey-Bird, shown here, *Scribner's* cover from 1899, "Sing A Song of Sixpence," "Alphabet," "Winter Sunrise, 1949," "The Reluctant Dragon," "Jack Sprat," and "A Swiss Admiral."

Scribner's Magazine

Headpiece to "It's Walls Were as of Jasper," by Kenneth Grahame. It appeared in the August, 1897 issue of *Scribner's*. The following pictures are from the same issue. *Parrish/Ludwig No. 099*

"Edward was the stalwart, bearded figure...who undauntedly discharged the fatal bullet into the shoulder of the great bison," page 160. *Parrish/Ludwig No. 102*

"A very fascinating background it was, and held a great deal, though so tiny," page 158. *Parrish/Ludwig No. 100*

"You could just see over the headland, and take in at your ease the life and bustle of the port," page 161. *Parrish/Ludwig No. 103*

"The hill on one side descended to water...and a very curly ship lay at anchor," page 159. *Parrish/Ludwig No. 101*

"As we eventually trundled off, it seemed to me an utter waste of that afternoon, could never be made up," page 162. *Parrish/Ludwig No. 104*

"A grave butler who...pretended to have entirely forgotten his familiar intercourse with me," page 163. *Parrish/Ludwig No. 105*

"When I got the book open, there was a difficulty at first in making the great stiff pages lie down," page 166. *Parrish/Ludwig No. 108*

"In ten seconds they had their heads together and were hard at talking clothes," page 164. *Parrish/Ludwig No. 106*

"From the deck I should see the little walled town recede and sink and grow slim," page 167. *Parrish/Ludwig No. 109*

"I glanced carefully around. They were still deep in clothes, both talking together," page 165. *Parrish/Ludwig No. 107*

Tailpiece from "Its Walls Were as of Jasper," page 168. *Parrish/Ludwig No. 110*

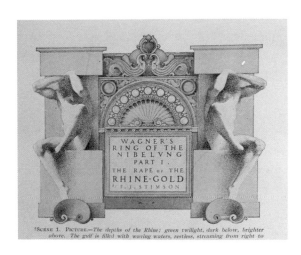

Illustrations and border designs for F.J. Stemson's "Wagner's Ring of Nibelung Part I: The Rape of the Rhine Gold," *Scribner's Magazine*, December, 1898. This is the headpiece. *Parrish/Ludwig No. 184*

Scribner's Magazine cover, Christmas Number, December, 1897. *Parrish/Ludwig No. 126*

"Alberich, the Dwarf," page 694. *Parrish/Ludwig No. 185*

Illustration for Grace Goodale's poem, "At An Amateur Pantomine," *Scribner's Magazine*, November, 1898. *Parrish/Ludwig No. 179*

"Alberich, the Dwarf," right panel, page 695. *Parrish/Ludwig No. 186*

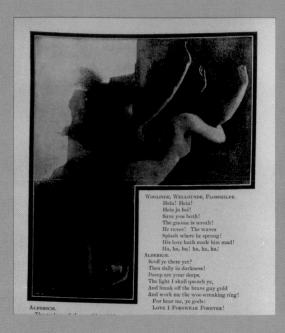

"Rhein Maidens and Alberich," left, page 698. *Parrish/Ludwig No. 189*

"Rhein Maidens and Alberich," right, page 699. *Parrish/Ludwig No. 190*

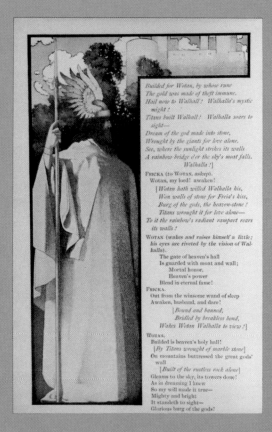

"Wotan Standing before Valhalla," left, page 700. *Parrish/Ludwig No. 191*

"Wotan Standing before Valhalla," right, page 701. *Parrish/Ludwig No. 192*

"Helmet Band" headpiece, page 702 and 703. *Parrish/Ludwig No. 196*

Headpiece, page 696. *Parrish/Ludwig No. 182*

Headpiece, page 697. *Parrish/Ludwig No. 188*

Decorative border, page 704. *Parrish/Ludwig No. 198*

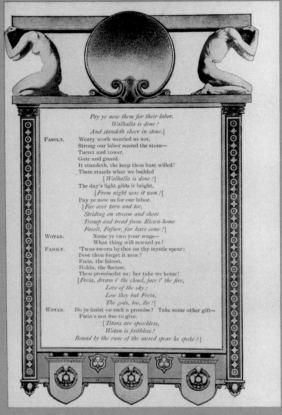

Decorative border, page 705. *Parrish/Ludwig No. 199*

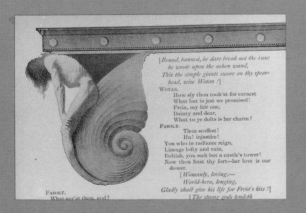

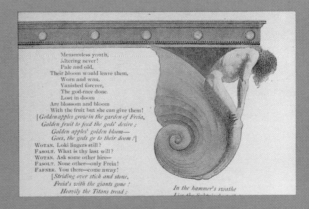

Headpiece, pages 706 and 707. *Parrish/Ludwig No. 200*

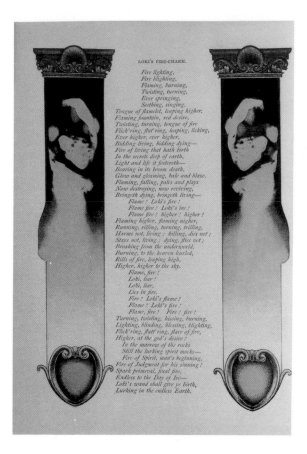

"Loki's Fire Charm," page 708. *Parrish/Ludwig No. 197*

Scribner's Magazine cover, August, 1899. *Parrish/Ludwig No. 212*

Scribner's Magazine cover, April, 1899. *Parrish/Ludwig No. 206*

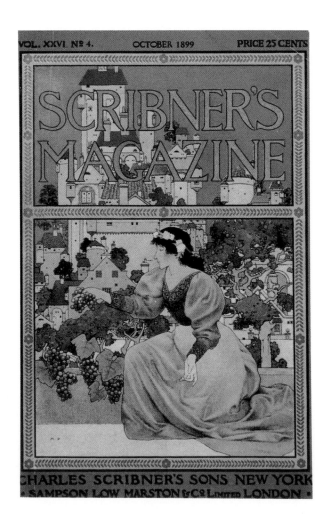

Scribner's Magazine, cover, October, 1899. *Parrish/Ludwig No. 217*

Headpiece for "The Duchess at Prayer," page 151. *Parrish/Ludwig No. 268*

"The duchess' apartments are beyond,' said the old man," page 152. *Parrish/Ludwig No. 270*

"He was the kind of man who brings a sour mouth to the eating of the sweetest apple," page 161. *Parrish/Ludwig No. 271*

Scribner's Magazine cover, Christmas Number, December, 1899. *Parrish/Ludwig No. 216*

"They were always together…walking in the gardens," illustration for Edith Wharton's "The Duchess at Prayer," *Scribner's Magazine, August, 1900, page 150. Parrish/Ludwig No. 267*

Tailpiece to "The Duchess at Prayer," page 163.

Scribner's Magazine cover, October, 1900. *Parrish/Ludwig No. 081*

Illustration for the Josephine Preston Peabody's poem, "Play Up,
Piper," *Scribner's Magazine, August, 1900. Parrish/Ludwig No. 264*

Scribner's Magazine cover, Christmas Number, December, 1900.
Parrish/Ludwig No. 275

Illustrations for A.T. Quiller-Couch's "Phoebus on Halzaphron," *Scribner's Magazine*, August, 1901. This is the headpiece from page 163. *Parrish/Ludwig No. 289*

"The rolling downs were not, but in their place a bright line," page 165. *Parrish/Ludwig No. 287*

"Through the night she calls to men, luring them down to their death," page 167. *Parrish/Ludwig No. 309*

"And their king...watched...their dark sails moving out against the sunset," page 166. *Parrish/Ludwig No. 285*

"One black noon in November a company of men crossed the sands at low water and demanded to speak with the King," pages 168-169. *Parrish/Ludwig No. 286*

"And drew aside behind a rock while they passed," page 172. *Parrish/Ludwig No. 310*

Tailpiece for "Phoebus on Halzaphron," *Scribner's Magazine,* August, 1901. *Parrish/Ludwig No. 290*

"Twilight had fallen before the stranger rose and took his farewell," pages 170-171. *Parrish/Ludwig No. 283* (left) and *Parrish/Ludwig No. 284* (right)

Scribner's Magazine cover, Christmas Number, December, 1901. *Parrish/Ludwig No. 302*

"The Cardinal Archbishop Sat on his Shaded Balcony," frontispiece for "The Turquoise Cup", *Scribner's Magazine*, December, 1901, page 671. *Parrish/Ludwig No. 311*

By Arthur Cosslett Smith

Headpiece for "The Turquoise Cup," by Arthur Cosslett Smith. *Scribner's Magazine*, December, 1901. *Parrish/Ludwig No. 313*

"he...drew out two flowers, one withered, the other fresh," a frontispiece for "The Desert," *Scribner's Magazine*, December, 1902. *Parrish/Ludwig No. 338*

"Lady Nora and the Cardinal at St. Marks," illustration for "The Turquoise Cup," *Scribner's Magazine*, December, 1901, page 689. *Parrish/Ludwig No. 312*

"Aucassin Seeks for Nicolette," a frontispiece for A.M. Davis Ogden's "Romance," *Scribner's Magazine*, July, 1902. *Parrish/Ludwig No. 307*

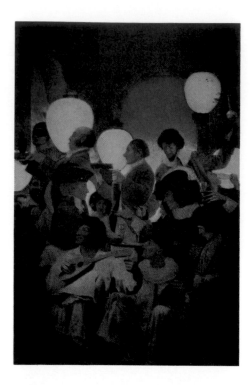

"The two young men were presently hobnobbing over a glass of canary," frontispiece for "A Venetian Night's Entertainment," *Scribner's Magazine*, December, 1903. *Parrish/Ludwig No. 351*

Frontispiece for William Lucius Graves' "The Vigil-at-Arms," *Scribner's Magazine*, December, 1904. *Parrish/Ludwig No. 560*

Scribner's Magazine cover, October, 1904. *Parrish/Ludwig No. 559*

"Ah never in this world were there such a rose/As once from that enchanted trellis hung," frontispiece illustration for H.G. Dwight's "Potpourri," *Scribner's Magazine*, August, 1905. *Parrish/Ludwig No. 389*

"Venice-Twilight," frontispiece illustration for Arthur Symons'
"The Waters of Venice," *Scribner's Magazine*, April, 1906.
Parrish/Ludwig No. 390

"No more 'mid low Achaean hills/Echo the flutes of Pan,"
frontispiece illustration for George T. Marsh's "The Errant Pan,"
Scribner's Magazine, August, 1910. *Parrish/Ludwig No. 582*

"On the other side of the water Venice begins," illustration for
"The Waters of Venice." *Parrish/Ludwig No. 391*

"Old Romance," *Scribner's Magazine*, August, 1907. According to
Ludwig, this was originally drawn for a *Women's Home Companion*
competition in 1907. *Parrish/Ludwig No. 569*

"Let's Pretend the Parting Hour Never More Shall Find Us,"
illustration for Rosamund Marriott Watson's "Make-Believe,"
Scribner's Magaaine, August, 1912. Also known as "Land of Make
Believe." *Parrish/Ludwig No. 562*

The prospectus for *Scribner's Magazine*, 1898. *Parrish/Ludwig No. 140*

Scribner's Magazine cover, Fiction Number, August, 1923. This first appeared as a Scribner's poster in 1897. *Parrish/Ludwig No. 117*

The cover for the program of the 1897 "Scribner Christmas Dinner." Ludwig reports that the art work was done gratis for J.H. Chapin. *Parrish/Ludwig No. 169*

Cover and title page from *Scribner's Magazine's* prospectus for 1900. *Parrish/Ludwig No. 539 & Parrish/Ludwig No. 540*

"Scribner's Books for Younger Readers," featuring "The Fly-Away Horse". *Parrish/Ludwig No. 374*

VIM

VIM was an in-house publication for Curtis Publishing. This March, 1927 edition feature a variation on "Air Castles" with the bubbles filled with other, non-Parrish, images. *Parrish/Ludwig No. 557*

Success

Success cover, Christmas Number, December, 1901. *Parrish/Ludwig No. 301*

Yankee Magazine

Yankee Magazine cover, "White Birch in Winter," December, 1935. *Parrish/Ludwig No. 755*

Covers and Programs for Non-Commercial Institutions

The young Maxfield Parrish did a lot of work around the Philadelphia area creating covers, programs, and other items for the local colleges and clubs. Among his earliest works was the cover for the *Bryn Mawr College Lantern*, done in 1891. In addition to the work for Bryn Mawr, he designed items for his alma mater, Haverford College, the Pennsylvania Academy of the Fine Arts, the West Chester Cricket Club, and The Mask and Wig Club of the University of Pennsylvania. The tap room of the Mask and Wig Club is something of a shrine to Parrish lovers. It is still dominated by the mural of "Old King Cole," and many of the caricature's above the mug hooks are from Parrish's hands. It is an added delight to see that the caricature tradition has continued to this day.

The early work for some of these organizations led quite naturally into Parrish's commercial work.

Parrish designed the decorative artwork for this invitation to the Junior Exercises of the Class of 1992, which was held at Alumni Hall on Thursday, April 16th, 1891. *Parrish/Ludwig No. not assigned*

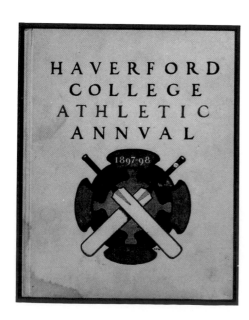

Haverford College Athletic Annual cover, 1898. *Parrish/Ludwig No.*

Haverford Verse cover, 1908. *Parrish/Ludwig No. 511*

"No Gentlemen of France" program cover, The Mask and Wig Club, University of Pennsylvania, 1896. *Parrish/Ludwig No. 046*

"Kenilworth" program cover, The Mask and Wig Club, University of Pennsylvania, 1895. Interestingly Parrish has signed the piece "F. Maxfield Parrish," a use of his first initial (for Frederick) which he seems to have dropped by the time of the next year's program. *Parrish/Ludwig No. 022*

"Jefferson Theatre Program," Portland, Maine, for 1905 and 1906, published by A.H. Dunn Co. 1905. *Parrish/Ludwig No. not assigned*

Posters & Advertisements

Ludwig makes note that "Parrish regarded most of his advertisement designs as posters and referred to them by that term." (page 531) Following that precept we have included together in this chapter, with posters first and advertising second. For the collector, the poster form is most desireable and it is among the most rare.

Advertising takes many forms, and Parrish's images have been used in a variety of ways, from newspapers to billboards. Most of the advertisements may also be found in publications other than those listed. Edison Mazda advertisements have been organized at the end of the Edison Mazda calendar material in the following section, and there are some items in the miscellaneous section that some might say should be here. Alas, the division of such things is not always easy.

Adlake Camera

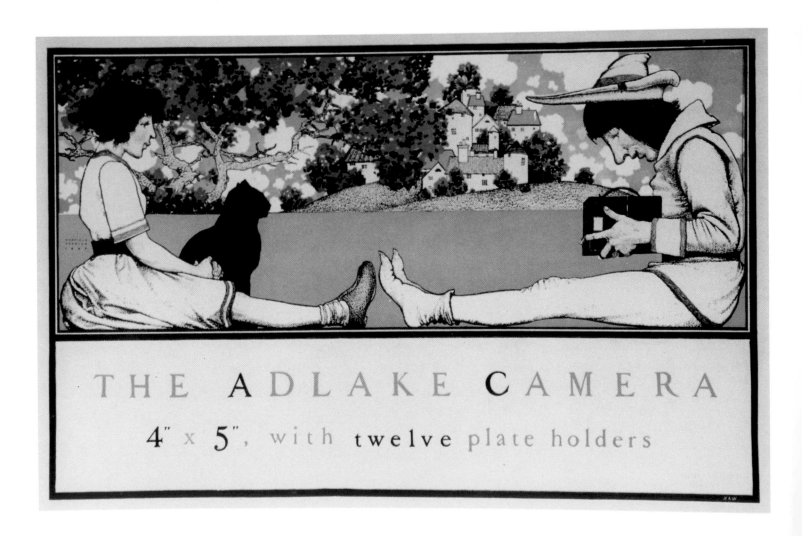

"The Adlake Camera" poster, 1897. *Parrish/Ludwig No. 170*

Book News

Poster for *Book News,* October 1895. *Parrish/Ludwig No. 020*

American Water Color Society

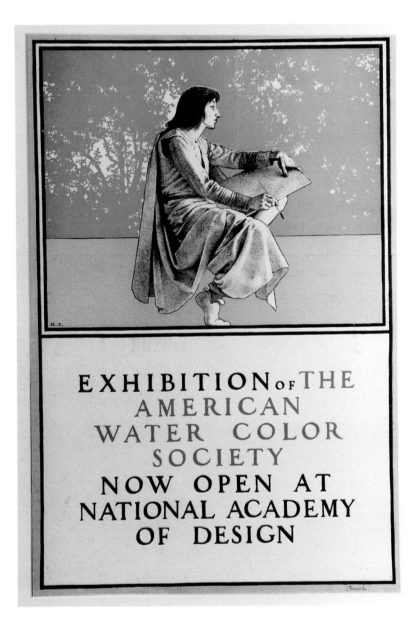

Poster for the American Water Color Society's exhibition at the National Academy of Design, 1899. 22″ x 14½″. *Parrish/Ludwig No. 208*

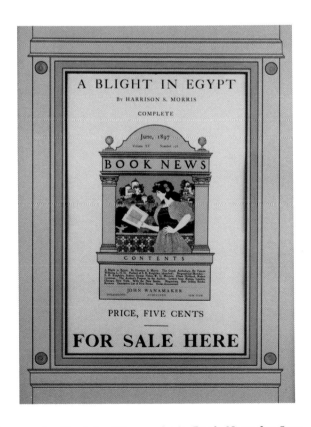

Store poster for John Wanamaker's *Book News* for June, 1897. *Parrish/Ludwig No. 097*

Century Magazine

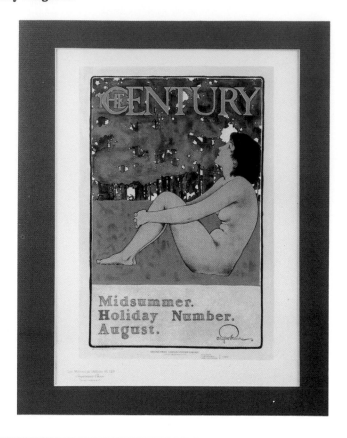

Poster for *Century* magazine's Midsummer Holiday Number. Parrish won second prize ($75) for this submission to a poster contest. He was one of 700 competitors. This reprint from the September 1897 issue of *The Inland Painter* has no date and has the artist's signature in the lower right hand corner. Original size when drawn 31½" x 22". *Parrish/Ludwig No. 052*

Colgate & Company

Colgate & Company poster designed by Parrish. The Dutch boy became a symbol of the company's products, including Cashmere Bouquet. 1897. 10½" x 15¼". *Parrish/Ludwig No. 087*

Poster for *Century Magazine's* May, 1902 issue featuring "The Great Southwest" with Parrish's illustrations. *Parrish/Ludwig No. 317*

Davis Theatre

Ferry Company

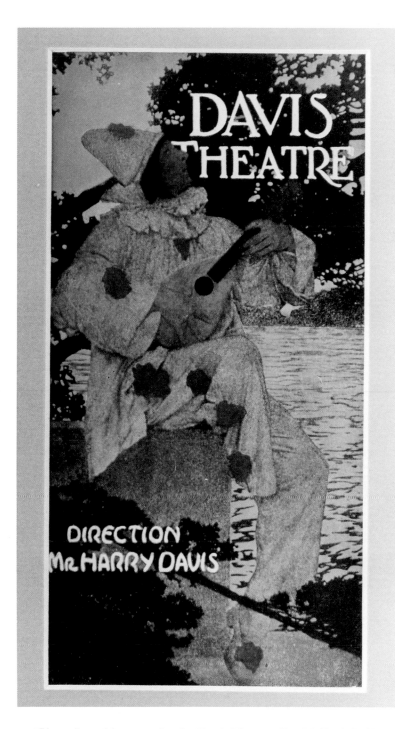

"Peter, Peter, Pumpkin Eater" poster, 1918, for the D.M. Ferry Seed Company, Detroit, Michigan. *Parrish/Ludwig No. 642*

"Pierrot" on this poster for the Davis Theatre. *Parrish/Ludwig No. 461*

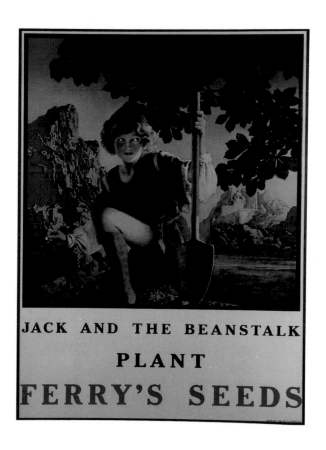

"Jack and the Beanstalk" poster for the D.M. Ferry Seed Company, Detroit, Michigan, 1923. *Parrish/Ludwig No. 688*

"Peter Piper picked a peck of pickled peppers" poster for D.M. Ferry
Seed Company, 1920. *Parrish/Ludwig No. 622*

Harper's Weekly

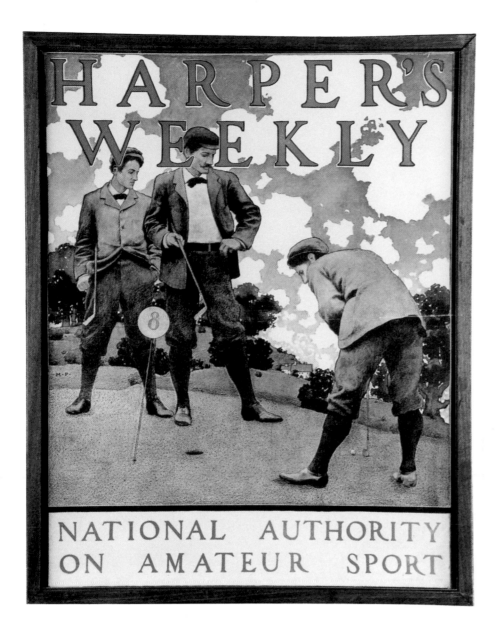

Harper's Weekly, "National Authority on Amateur Sports" poster, 1897. *Parrish/Ludwig No. 115*

Life

A *Life* poster featuring the cover of its March 1, 1923 issue, "A Dark Futurist," 10¾″ x 15½″. *Parrish/Ludwig No. 684*

M-P Productions

Los Angeles Municipal Arts Department

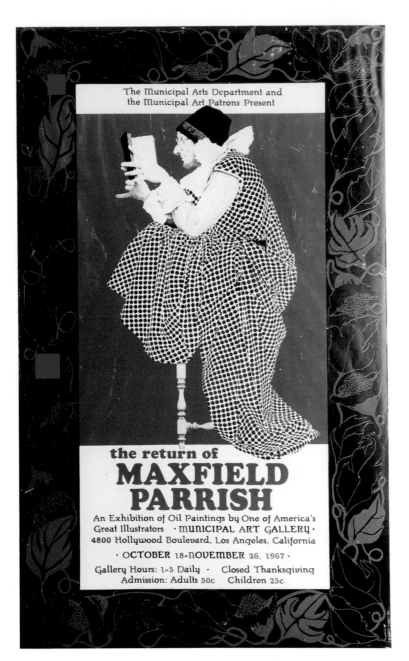

M-P Productions poster for "Maxfield Parrish Nights" commemorating the opening of the Maxfield Parrish Museum in 1978. The image is identified as "Ex Libris—Circa 1923 —A Maxfield Parrish Mirage," which was donated by Les Allen Ferry. *Parrish/Ludwig No. not assigned*

Maxfield Parrish Museum

"The Idiot" or "The Book Lover" graces this poster for Los Angeles Municipal Arts Departments exhibition of Parrish Oils, "The Return of Maxfield Parrish." It was held at the Municipal Art Gallery from October 18 to December 26, 1967. *Parrish/Ludwig No. 583*

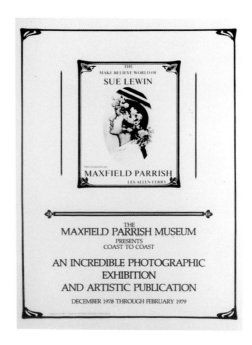

This is poster for an exhibition of Maxfield Parrish's photographs of his friend, sometimes housekeeper, and ofttimes model, Sue Lewin. It was held at the Maxfield Parrish Museum from December, 1978 through February, 1979. The poster is copyrighted by Les Allen Ferry and funded by the Friends of Maxfield Parrish Society.

New Hampshire Planning and Development Commission

The New Hampshire Scenic Planning and Development Commission used posters to promote growth and tourism in the state, 1936. The small print at the bottom of this "Land of Scenic Splendor" poster indicates that Parrish painted the image specially for the Planning and Development Commission, and that he is a native son, living in Cornish, New Hampshire. It also indicates that the poster could be purchased for one dollar. The image is also known as "Thy Templed Hills" and used by Brown & Bigelow for a calendar, 1942. *Parrish/Ludwig No. 760*

No-To-Bac

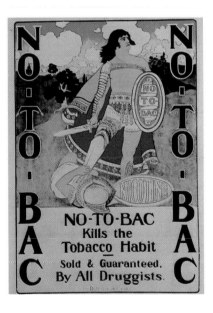

This "No-To-Bac" image was originally a 29″ x 13¾″ poster published in 1896. This is a postcard size version of the same. Published by the Dando Printers, Philadelphia. *Parrish/Ludwig No. 053*

"New Hampshire: The Winter Paradise" was also made specially for the New Hampshire Planning and Development Commission, 1939, to use in this poster. *Parrish/Ludwig No. 769*

Pennsylvania Academy of the Fine Arts

Scribner's Magazine

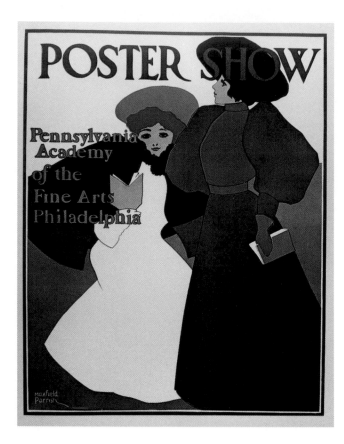

The image from Parrish's poster for the Pennsylvania Academy of the Fine Arts "Poster Show." The whole poster had writing at the bottom which read, "Paintings of the Glasgow School/Fosdick's Fire Etchings/Academy of Fine Arts". Overall size 44″ x 28″. 1896. *Parrish/Ludwig No. 047*

Red Cross

"Scribner's Fiction Number. August" poster, 1897. *Parrish/Ludwig No. 117*

This design for the Red Cross appeared in *Art and the Great War* by A.E. Gallatin, 1919, with detail images. *Parrish/Ludwig No. 643*

"A Christmas Scribner's" poster promoting the December, 1897 issue which had a "Special Christmas Cover in 9 colors by Maxfield Parrish." 19½" x 13½". *Parrish/Ludwig No. 159*

Poster advertising the April, 1899 issue of *Scribner's Magazine*. 21" x 14". *Parrish/Ludwig No. 206*

Success

Way and Williams

Poster for Baum's *Mother Goose in Prose,* Way and Williams, Publishers, 1897. *Parrish/Ludwig No. 135*

Poster for *Success* magazine featuring the cover of its December, 1901 issue. 10" x 14½". *Parrish/Ludwig No. 301*

Brill Brothers

Poster stamp for Brill Brothers.

Broadmoor Hotel

A cookie tin using the image of the Broadmoor Hotel in Colorado Springs. Parrish created the painting circa 1925. This tin is for the Deer Park Company. *Parrish/Ludwig No. 667*

Brochure for the Broadmoor. *Parrish/Ludwig No. 667*

Parrish's Broadmoor made it into this advertisement for Maxwell House Coffee, which was served exclusively at the Hotel. The Ladies' Home Journal, July, 1925.

Colgate & Company

Columbia Bicycle

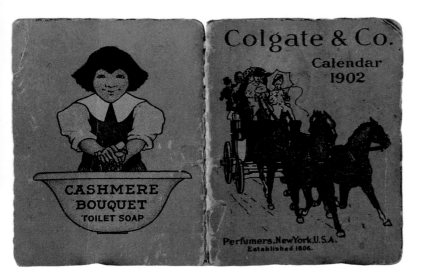

Small pocket calendar from Colgate & Company, 1902. *Parrish/Ludwig No. 087*

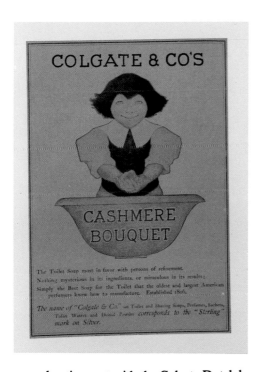

Newspaper advertisement with the Colgate Dutch boy.

Columbia Bicycle advertisement from designed for the back page of *Harper's Weekly*, April 11, 1896. *Parrish/Ludwig No. 045*

Crane

This design for Crane's Chocolates was used on candy boxes, advertising, and here on this poster stamp. *Parrish/Ludwig No. 618*

"The Rubaiyat" created for Crane's Chocolates in 1916, it is used on this highly decorated candy box. 1916. *Parrish/Ludwig No. 620*

"The Garden of Allah" illustration for Crane's Chocolate on this gessoed candy box, 1918. *Parrish/Ludwig No. 641*

Curtis Publishing

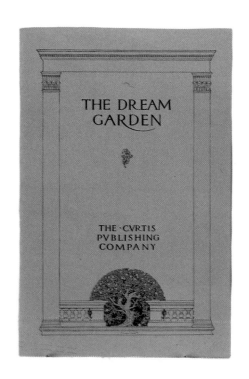

"The Dream Garden" brochure for Curtis Publishing Company, 1915 *Parrish/Ludwig No. 617*

Djer-Kiss

Advertisement for Djer-Kiss cosmetics featuring a girl and three elves, 1917. Appeared as an advertisement in *Ladies' Home Journal* in 1918. *Parrish/Ludwig No. 633*

Edison Mazda Lamps: see Edison Mazda Calendars.

"Mon Chef d'Ouevre..." Djer-Kiss advertisement appeared as a window card and as a magazine advertisement. c. 1916. *Parrish/Ludwig No. 621*

N.K. Fairbank Company

"Mon Chef d'Ouevre..." also appeared on this piece of promotional sheet music, the "Djer-Kiss Waltz" by Milton Ager. Published by Leo Feist, New York. *Parrish/Ludwig No. 621*

"Three of the greatest requisites of an enterprising housekeeper" advertisement for N.K. Fairbank Company soap products. This appeared in Harper's Bazar's March 28, 1896 issue, and promotes Cotco Bathsoap, Cottolene shortening, and Gold Dust Washing Powder. *Parrish/Ludwig No. 043*

Ferry Company

A small art print of "Peter, Peter, Pumpkin Eater" published by the Ferry Seed Company, 6¼" x 9¾". *Parrish/Ludwig No. 642*

The back cover of a seed catalog with "Peter, Peter, Pumpkin Eater" published by the Ferry Seed Company, 6¼" x 9¾". *Parrish/Ludwig No. 642*

Fisk Rubber Company

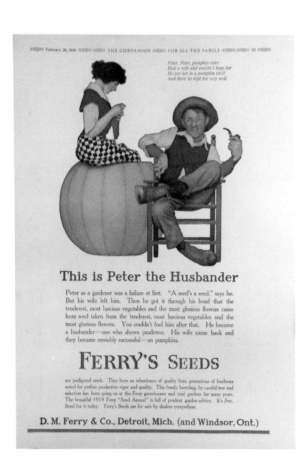

The "Peter, Peter..." graphic in a D.M. Ferry Seed advertisement which appeared in *The Companion for All the Family*, February 20, 1919. *Parrish/Ludwig No. 642*

"The Modern Magic Shoes" illustration for Fisk Tires. It was used extensively, including this advertisement in *Life* in 1917. *Parrish/Ludwig No. 634*

Another version of the "Fit for a King" advertisement. *Parrish/Ludwig No. 636*

"Magic Shoes" also graced the cover of the in house publication "The Fisker," September, 1917. It identifies the image as "a reproduction of an original painting made for the Fisk Rubber Company by Maxfield Parrish." *Parrish/Ludwig No. 634*

"Fit for a King" advertisement for Fisk Tires, 1917. Seeing the value of a Parrish illustration, the copy highlights it right beneath the title: "Reproduction of the famous painting made by Maxfield Parrish for the Fisk Rubber Company." *Parrish/Ludwig No. 636*

Detail of a large cut-out display of "Fit for a King." 11½" x 5" *Parrish/Ludwig No. 636*

Fisk Rubber Company also produced the "Mother Goose" image as an art print, suitable for framing. *Parrish/Ludwig No. 649*

"Mother Goose" advertisement for Fisk Tires. This appeared in the August, 1919 issue of *Country Life* magazine. *Parrish/Ludwig No. 649*

The popularity of the "Mother Goose" illustration can be seen in its use as a wallpaper border, published by Fisk Rubber Company. The advertising is gone, but the tire remains as a subtle reminder of the goodness of Fisk Tire to provide such a nice decoration. *Parrish/Ludwig No. 649*

"The Magic Circle" advertisement for Fisk Tires, 1919. This is the magazine version, but the image appeared in many forms. *Parrish/Ludwig No. 650*

Genesee Pure Food Company

Genesee Pure Food Company introduced this Jell-o advertisement in 1921. *Parrish/Ludwig No. 666*

The backside of the wallpaper with instructions for its application.

"Polly Put the Kettle On" advertisement for Jell-o, the Genesee Pure Food Company, 1923. *Parrish/Ludwig No. 686*

Charles E. Hires Company

The figure to the right of the caldron was cut out to produce this magazine advertisement "Just say Hires. *Parrish/Ludwig No. 657*

Oneida Community

"Ask for Hires and get the genuine" advertisement for Hires Root Beer, the Charles E. Hires Company, Philadelphia, 1920. The image was used in many ways to promote Hires. *Parrish/Ludwig No. 657*

"Community Plate" advertisement for Oneida Silver appeared in *The Ladies' Home Journal*, December, 1918. The banner at the bottom reads "Painted by Maxfield Parrish for Oneida Community." *Parrish/Ludwig No. 637*

Pettijohn's Breakfast Food

"Little Boy Blue" from *Mother Goose in Prose* can be found in the upper corner of this advertisement for Pettijohn's Breakfast Food. The ad offers a copy of the book to those who send in the three bears from one box of Pettijohn's plus 8 cents for postage. *Parrish/Ludwig No. 166*

Royal Baking Powder

"Royal Baking Powder Makes Dainties for Christmas" advertisement from the back cover of *Harper's Weekly, December 14, 1895. Parrish/Ludwig No. 538*

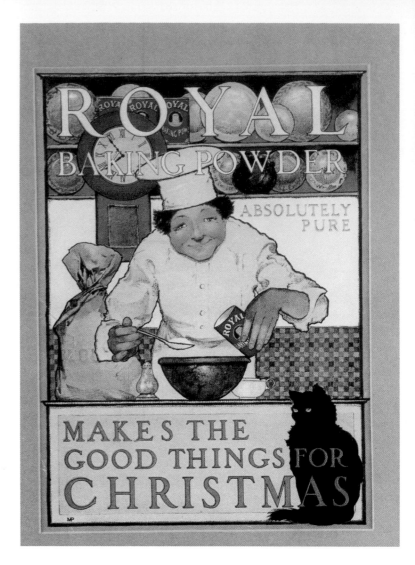

"Royal Baking Powder Makes Good Things for Christmas" from the back of Scribner's Magazine, December, 1897. *Parrish/Ludwig No. 133*

Royal Baking Powder advertisement from the back cover of *Scribner's Magazine*, December, 1900. *Parrish/Ludwig No. 280*

Sterling Bicycle

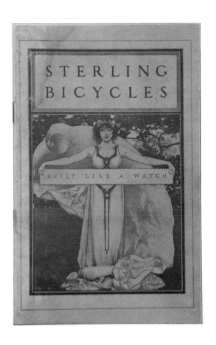

"Sterling Bicycles: Built Like a Watch" catalog, 1897. *Parrish/Ludwig No. 168*

The Parrish baker image is altered slightly for use in this Royal Baking Powder advertisement. The alteration and the background was probably done by an artist other than Parrish. *Parrish/Ludwig No. 315*

Swift and Company

"Royal Baking Powder Makes the Cook's Work Easy and Delicious Food Certain," advertisement from *Scribner's Magazine*, December 1901. *Parrish/Ludwig No. 315*

Swift's Premium Ham "Jack Sprat" advertisement, which appeared in the November, 1921 issue of *Ladies' Home Journal*. Swift and Company. *Parrish/Ludwig No. 646*

The Tea Tray

"The Tea Tray." Parrish made a two-sided sign for a friend's tea shop in New Hampshire. The two sides of the sign are reproduced on postcards copyrighted by M. Parker. Original size was about four feet long. *Parrish/Ludwig No. 771*

The reverse side of "The Tea Tray," also from a Parker postcard. *Parrish/Ludwig No. 772*

Vermont Association for Billboard Restriction

"Buy Products Not Advertised on our Road Sides," 1939. This image was done for the Vermont Association for Billboard Restriction and was issued as a poster and as this postcard. The postcard was sold by the Association and by the National Roadside Council for two cents.

John Wanamaker

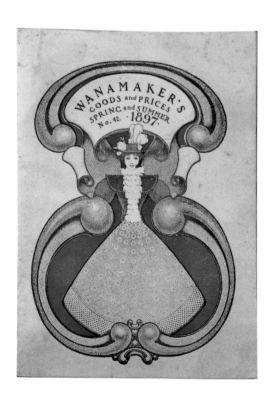

"Wanamaker's Goods and Prices, Spring and Summer, No. 42, 1897" catalog cover. *Parrish/Ludwig No. 079*

Brown & Bigelow and Edison Mazda: Calendars and More

We separate calendars from advertisements for the convenience of the collector. In fact, most calendars shown here are a very clever sort of advertising, keeping the advertisers name before the public for a whole year.

Brown & Bigelow used Parrish images in a variety of ways, and still holds the copyright to many of the images. The calendars came in a variety of sizes, each bearing a Parrish landscape or winterscape, and, usually, the advertising of a company that gave them to its customers.

The winterscapes were introduced in the early 1940s, and were used on a second line of calendars and on greeting cards for the holidays.

General Electric used Parrish images in their advertising from 1918 to 1934. The calendars came in a small and large size (except for 1932 when only the small size was produced), and the images found their way into other forms of General Electric advertising as well.

Brown & Bigelow Landscapes

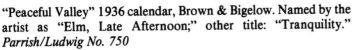

"Peaceful Valley" 1936 calendar, Brown & Bigelow. Named by the artist as "Elm, Late Afternoon;" other title: "Tranquility." *Parrish/Ludwig No. 750*

"Twilight" blotter, 1937, Brown & Bigelow. Overall size, 4″ x 9″. *Parrish/Ludwig No. 758*

"The Glen" printer's proof. This image was kept as a reference to check the correctness of color when Brown & Bigelow reprinted it. It appeared on their 1938 calendar. *Parrish/Ludwig No. 765*

"Twilight" large calendar top, 1937, Brown & Bigelow. Size: 16½" x 22". *Parrish/Ludwig No. 758*

"Early Autumn" printer's proof. This image was used on the 1939 Brown & Bigelow calendar. Parrish named it "Autumn Brook." *Parrish/Ludwig No. 766*

"Evening Shadows" large calendar top, 1940, Brown & Bigelow. Named "The Old Birch Tree" by the artist. *Parrish/Ludwig No. 768*

"Thy Templed Hills" large calendar top, Brown & Bigelow, 1942. Also known as "New Hampshire: The Land of Scenic Splendor." *Parrish/Ludwig No. 760*

"The Village Brook" 1941 Brown & Bigelow Calendar. Overall size: 16″ x 22″. *Parrish/Ludwig No. 770*

"A Perfect Day" calendar top, Brown & Bigelow, 1943. Also known as "June Skies." *Parrish/Ludwig No. 776*

"Thy Rocks and Rills" or "The Old Mill," Brown & Bigelow calendar, 1944. *Parrish/Ludwig No. 782*

"Thy Rocks and Rills" printer's proof for color accuracy. *Parrish/Ludwig No. 782*

"Sunup," 1945 calendar top, Brown & Bigelow. Also known as "Little Brook Farm." *Parrish/Ludwig No. 791*

"Evening" calendar top, 1947, Brown & Bigelow. *Parrish/Ludwig No. 794*

"Valley of Enchantment" calendar, Brown & Bigelow, 1946. *Parrish/Ludwig No. 785*

"The Mill Pond," Brown & Bigelow calendar, 1948. *Parrish/Ludwig No. 795*

"The Village Church," Brown & Bigelow calendar top, 1949. *Parrish/Ludwig No. 799*

"Daybreak" or "Hunt Farm" printers' proof for the Brown & Bigelow calendar for 1951. *Parrish/Ludwig No. 807*

"Sunlit Valley," Brown & Bigelow calendar, 1950. *Parrish/Ludwig No. 803*

"An Ancient Tree," Brown & Bigelow calendar top, 1952. *Parrish/Ludwig No. 809*

"Evening Shadows," Brown & Bigelow calendar, 1953. Parrish named this piece "Peace of Evening." *Parrish/Ludwig No. 823*

"Peaceful Valley," Brown & Bigelow calendar, 1955. Also known as "Homestead." *Parrish/Ludwig No. 828*

"The Old Glen Mill" Brown & Bigelow calendar, 1954. The painting is also known as "Glen Mills." *Parrish/Ludwig No. 826*

"Misty Morn," 1956 calendar, Brown & Bigelow. Parrish called this image "Swift-Water." *Parrish/Ludwig No. 832*

"Morning Light," 1957 Brown & Bigelow calendar. The image is also known as "The Little Stone House." *Parrish/Ludwig No. 834*

A smaller version of the 1956 "Misty Morn" calendar. *Parrish/Ludwig No. 832*

Smaller version of the 1957 "Morning Light" calendar. *Parrish/Ludwig No. 834*

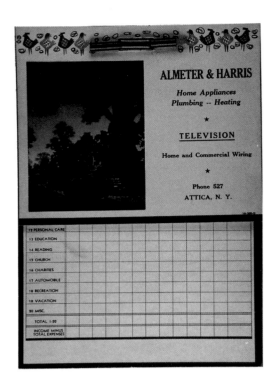

Hanging budget keeper with "Morning Light" image. *Parrish/Ludwig No. 834*

"Under Summer Skies" calendar top, Brown & Bigelow, 1959. *Parrish/Ludwig No. 840* The image is also known as "Janion's Maple."

"New Moon," 1958 calendar, Brown & Bigelow. *Parrish/Ludwig No. 838*

"Sheltering Oaks" 1960 Brown & Bigelow calendar with their own advertising. The image is also known as "A Nice Place to Be." *Parrish/Ludwig No. 841*

A printer's proof for "Sheltering Oaks." This was carefully stored at Brown & Bigelow to be used as a color reference whenever the image was reprinted. *Parrish/Ludwig No. 841*

The printer's proof for "Quiet Solitude" the image in Brown & Bigelow's 1962 calendar. This image is also known as "Cascades." *Parrish/Ludwig No. 847*

"Twilight," the top from the 1961 Brown & Bigelow calendar. The image is also known as "The White Oak." *Parrish/Ludwig No. 844*

"Peaceful Country" calendar proof for the 1963 Brown & Bigelow calendar. *Parrish/Ludwig No. 849*

Playing cards, published by Brown & Bigelow. They were used by Brown & Bigelow salesman, Lee Murri, as a giveaway to his customers. On the left is "Sheltering Oaks" and on the right is "New Moon." *Parrish/Ludwig No. 838 and 841*

Brown & Bigelow Winterscapes

"Winter Twilight" on a Christmas card. This image, which Parrish called "Tranquility," was published as an executive print. Brown & Bigelow, 1941. *Parrish/Ludwig No. 812*

"Silent Night," executive print, Brown & Bigelow, 1942. Artist's title: "Winter Night." *Parrish/Ludwig No. 777*

"Eventide," executive print, Brown & Bigelow, 1944. *Parrish/Ludwig No. 783*

"At Close of Day," Brown & Bigelow, 1943. Parrish called this image "Plainfield N.H. Church at Dusk" and it was published as an executive print. *Parrish/Ludwig No. 778*

"Silent Night" or "Lights of Home," Christmas card. Brown & Bigelow, 1945. This was also printed as an executive print. *Parrish/Ludwig No. 786*

"The Path to Home" executive print, 1946. Parrish called this image "Across the Valley." *Parrish/Ludwig No. 793*

"Christmas Morning," executive print, Brown & Bigelow, 1949. *Parrish/Ludwig No. 784*

"Peace at Twilight" executive print, 1947. Parrish named it "Lull Brook." *Parrish/Ludwig No. 797*

"A New Day" executive print, Brown & Bigelow, 1950. Called "Afterglow" by Parrish. *Parrish/Ludwig No. 804*

"Christmas Eve," 1948, executive print from the Brown & Bigelow. Parrish named this image "Deep Valley." *Parrish/Ludwig No. 798*

"The Twilight Hour," Brown & Bigelow, 1951. The image on this Christmas card also graced an executive print. Parrish called it "Hilltop Farm, Winter." *Parrish/Ludwig No. 820*

"Peaceful Night" executive print, Brown & Bigelow, 1953. Named "Church at Norwich" by Parrish. *Parrish/Ludwig No. 824*

"Lights of Welcome" art print, Brown & Bigelow, 1952. According to Ludwig, Parrish also called this image "Hilltop Farm, Winter." *Parrish/Ludwig No. 810*

"When Day is Dawning" executive print, Brown & Bigelow, 1954. Named "Winter Sunrise" by Parrish. *Parrish/Ludwig No. 827*

"Sunrise" executive print, Brown & Bigelow, 1955. Parrish called this image, "White Birches in a Glow." *Parrish/Ludwig No. 829*

"Evening" executive print, Brown & Bigelow, 1956. *Parrish/Ludwig No. 833*

"A Christmas Morning" Christmas card, Brown & Bigelow, 1958. This image appeared as an executive print. It has been named "Sunlight," and Parrish called it "Winter Sunshine." *Parrish/Ludwig No. 839*

"At Close of Day" excecutive print, Brown & Bigelow, 1957. Named "Norwich, Vermont" by Parrish. *Parrish/Ludwig No. 835*

"Peace of Evening" executive print, Brown & Bigelow, 1959. Named "Dingleton Farm" by Parrish. *Parrish/Ludwig No. 842*

"Evening Shadows" Christmas card, Brown & Bigelow, 1962. This was the image on an art print. *Parrish/Ludwig No. 848*

P.F. Collier and Son

"The Calendar of Cheer," Dodge Publishing, 1926. "Prince Codadad." *Parrish/Ludwig No. 419*

Advertisement for the Maxfield Parrish Art Calendar for 1907 with the graphic "Summer." Other illustrations in this calendar were "Father Time," "Spring," and "Harvest." Each was printed in five colors and the calendar measured 15" x 21". *Parrish/Ludwig No. 404*

Dodge Publishing Company

"The Contentment Calendar," Dodge Publishing, 1926, with "Summer" graphic. *Parrish/Ludwig No. 404*

Two Dodge Publishing calendars. Left: "Calendar of Sunshine" featuring the "Quest of Golden Fleece." *Parrish/Ludwig No. 457* Right: "Sunshine Calendar" with "Singing Tree." *Parrish/Ludwig No. 415*

"Jason and the Talking Oak," on this 1925 Calendar of Friendship,   Dodge Publishing. *Parrish/Ludwig No. 452*

Thomas Murphy Co.

"When Winter Comes" on Thomas Murphy Co. 1941 calendar. Parrish's signature has the date 1931 beside it. This image was entitled "White Birch—Winter" when it appeared on *Yankee Magazine's* cover in 1935. *Parrish/Ludwig No. 755*

Edison Mazda Calendars and Advertising

"Dawn," the first calendar Maxfield Parrish created for the Mazda Lamp Works of the General Electric Company, 1918. Large version. *Parrish/Ludwig No. 638*

"Spirit of the Night," the large version of the 1919 calendar.
Parrish/Ludwig No. 644

"Prometheus," 1920 Edison Mazda calendar, large version.
Parrish/Ludwig No. 651

"Primitive Man," 1921 Edison Mazda calendar, large version. *Parrish/Ludwig No. 656*

Small version of the 1921 "Primitive Man" calendar. *Parrish/Ludwig No. 656*

"Egypt," Edison Mazda calendar for 1922. Large version. *Parrish/Ludwig No. 658*

"The Lamp Seller of Bagdad" calendar for Edison Mazda, 1923. Large version. *Parrish/Ludwig No. 689*

"Venetian Lamplighter" calendar for Edison Mazda, 1924. Large version. *Parrish/Ludwig No. 683*

"Dream Light," Edison Mazda calendar, 1925. Large version. *Parrish/Ludwig No. 715*

"Dreamlight" calendar, 1925, small version. *Parrish/Ludwig No. 715*

"Enchantment," 1926 calendar. Edison Mazda, large version.
Parrish/Ludwig No. 600

The smaller "Enchantment" calendar of 1926. *Parrish/Ludwig No. 600*

"Reveries," 1927 Edison Mazda calendar, large version. *Parrish/ Ludwig No. 723*

"Contentment," 1928 Edison Mazda calendar, large version.
Parrish/Ludwig No. 724

"Golden Hours." 1929 Edison Mazda calendar. Large version.
Parrish/Ludwig No. 726

"Golden Hours." 1929 Edison Mazda calendar, small version. *Parrish/Ludwig No. 726*

"Ecstasy." Large 1930 Edison Mazda calendar. *Parrish/Ludwig No. 728*

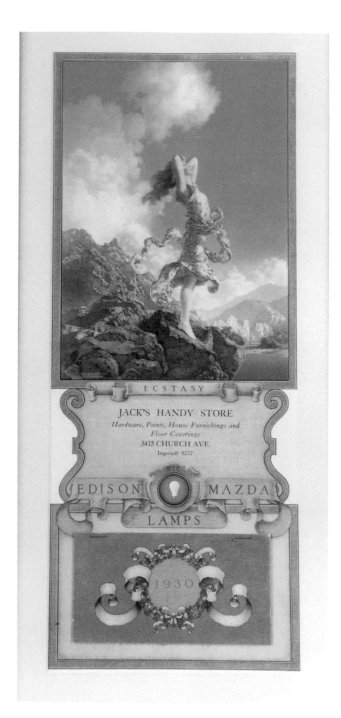

Smaller 1930 "Ecstasy" calendar. *Parrish/Ludwig No. 728*

"Waterfall," 1931 Edison Mazda calendar. Large version.
Parrish/Ludwig No. 735

Smaller 1931 "Waterfall" calendar. *Parrish/Ludwig No. 735*

1932 "Solitude" calendar. Small size. Edison Mazda. *Parrish/Ludwig No. 740*

"Sunrise." Small Edison Mazda calendar for 1933. *Parrish/Ludwig No. 742*

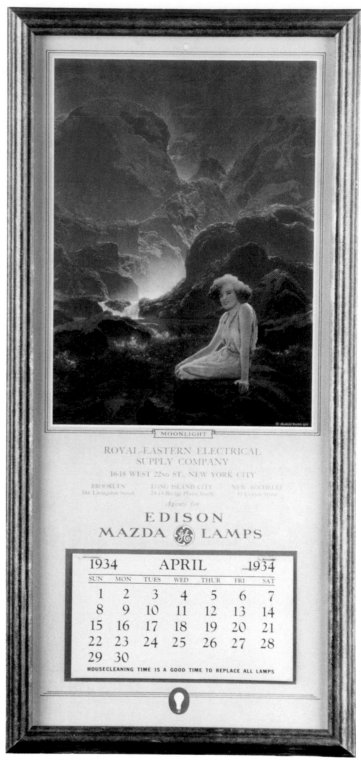

"Moonlight." 1934 Edison Mazda Calendar. Only issued in the small size, with a printing of 750,000. *Parrish/Ludwig No. 744*

Mailing tubes for Edison Mazda Calendars.

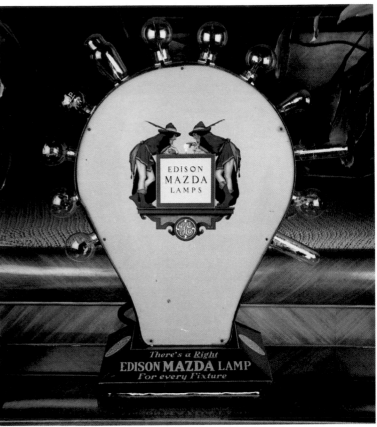

Lighted Mazda sign, for displaying lamps. Tin, 23″ x 16″.
Parrish/Ludwig No. 669

Edison Mazda decal on glass with lead came border. "Egypt."
Parrish/Ludwig No. 658

Enamel sign for Edison Mazda car lamps and accessories.
Parrish/Ludwig No. 669

"Edison Mazda Lamps" display with the Parrish-designed logo.
Parrish/Ludwig No. 669

Beautiful enameled two-sided hanging Edison Mazda sign.
Parrish/Ludwig No. 669

Life-sized die-cut cardboard sign for Edison Mazda lamps.
Parrish/Ludwig No. 669

One of the Edison Mazda counter signs tracing the history of lighting. This fagot dates from the stone age. The Parrish image is "Primitive Man." *Parrish/Ludwig No. 656*

The third Edison Mazda counter sign features Parrish's "Venetian Lamplighter." *Parrish/Ludwig No. 683*

This Edison Mazda counter sign looks at 400 B.C. and the vegetable oil pottery lamp. The image is "The Lamp Seller of Bagdad." *Parrish/Ludwig No. 689*

The Edison Mazda logo designed by Parrish in the 1920s. *Parrish/Ludwig No. 669*

January 3. 1920 advertisement for Edison Mazda featuring the Prometheus painting done for the 1920 calendar. *Parrish/Ludwig No. 651*

Edison Mazda advertisement from the November 1, 1924 Saturday Evening post. *Parrish/Ludwig No. 669*

Edison Mazda advertisement which appeared in the Saturday Evening Post, January 8, 1921. Known as "Primitive Man" on the calendar of 1921, it seems to have a more appropriate title here: "Woman: Keeper of the Light." *Parrish/Ludwig No. 656*

Edison Mazda advertisement from 1925. *Parrish/Ludwig No. 669*

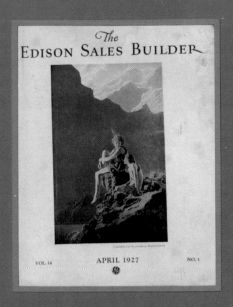

The *Edison Sales Builder* was an in-house organ of General Electric. This April, 1925 issue features "Enchantment." *Parrish/Ludwig No. 600*

Edison Sales Builder, May, 1926, featuring "Reveries." *Parrish/Ludwig No. 723*

"Contentment" on the cover of *Edison Sales Builder*, April, 1927. *Parrish/Ludwig No. 724*

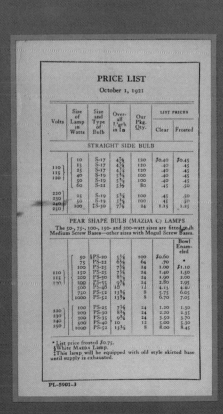

The April, 1930, *Edison Sales Builder,* with "Waterfall" on the cover. *Parrish/Ludwig No. 740*

Price list for Edison Mazda, featuring "Egypt" on cover. *Parrish/Ludwig No. 568*

EDISON MAZDA LAMPS

THE ELECTRIC HOSPITAL
K. B. Allured
47 Vernon St., Northampton, Mass.

"The Venetian Lamp-
lighter" on this Edison
Mazda blotter. Copyright
1924. 3½" x 6". *Parrish/
Ludwig No. 683*

EDISON
MAZDA
LAMPS

Good Lighting—the least expensive
of home comforts

W. H. BUTLER
Ludlow, Vermont.

Parrish's Edison Mazda logo
on this 1924 blotter. 3½" x 6".
Parrish/Ludwig No. 669

THE ELECTRIC HOSPITAL
K. B. Allured
47 Vernon St., Northampton, Mass.

"The Lamp Seller of Bagdad"
is featured on this Edison Mazda
advertising blotter. Copyright
1922. *Parrish/Ludwig No. 689*

A tape measure with Parrish's Edison Mazda
logo. *Parrish/Ludwig No. 669*

These ten decks of playing cards were
produced from 1918-1931, with images
corresponding to the images from each
year's calendar.

Art Prints

In the late 1800s a color craze swept America. With the perfection of color lithography, color images became more readily available at an affordable price, and Americans loved them. They collected every thing from trade cards and cigar labels, to magazine illustrations and pieces printed specifically to meet this desire.

Maxfield Parrish's work was among the most collectible, and in 1904 *The Ladies' Home Journal* offered "Air Castles" to its readers for a dime. Others followed, including *Scribner's* and *Collier's*, who reproduced Parrish's work in art print form.

As time passed Parrish garnered more control over the reproduction rights to his work, and began to reap more of its financial rewards. Eventually he was able to limit his advertising work and concentrate on art that was targetted to the home decorator. His collaboration with the House of Art produced some of his most beloved work, and that which collectors seek most avidly.

Bellerophon Watching by the Fountain
MAXFIELD PARRISH

"Bellerophon Watching by the Fountain," also known as "The Chimera" this print was included in a collection of "American Art by American Artists" along with ten other Parrish works, which was published by P.F. Collier & Son in 1914. *Parrish/Ludwig No. 455*

"Aucassin Seeks for Nicolette," 11½" x 17", Charles Scribner's Sons, 1903. *Parrish/Ludwig No. 307*

"The Broadmoor, Colorado Springs," art print, 1921, 19½" x 15".
Parrish/Ludwig No. 667

"The Broadmoor," small art print. *Parrish/Ludwig No. 667*

"Cadmus Sowing the Dragon's Teeth" art print, P.F. Collier & Son, 1909. Image size: 9¼" x 11½"; overall size: 11" x 13". Dodge Publishing Company, Detroit. *Parrish/Ludwig No. 420*

"Cassim in the Cave of the Forty Thieves" art print, P.F. Collier & Son, 1906. Part of a collection of "Maxfield Parrish's Four Best Paintings", which Collier issued. *Parrish/Ludwig No. 413*

"Circe's Palace," originally from *Tanglewood Tales: A Second Wonder Book*, it was part of the collection of "Maxfield Parrish's Four Best Paintings," published by P.F. Collier & Son, 1914. *Parrish/Ludwig No. 448*

"The Canyon," House of Art, 1924. 15″ x 12″. *Parrish/Ludwig No. 685*

"Cleopatra." This uncirculated print of "Cleopatra" shows the original colors. It bears the 1917 copyright of the Crane Candy Company, Cleveland, for whom it was originally painted. It was printed by Reinthal & Newman, New York. Small size, 6¼" x 7". *Parrish/Ludwig No. 632*

This is the medium size square cornered version of "Cleopatra" measuring 13½" x 15½" and printed by the House of Art. *Parrish/Ludwig No. 632*

"Daybreak," House of Art, 1923. This is the medium, 10″ x 18″ size.
Parrish/Ludwig No. 682

"The Dinkey-Bird," Charles Scribner's Sons, 1903. 16″ x 11″.
Parrish/Ludwig No. 378

"Dreaming," House of Art, 1928. Small 6″ x 10″ size. *Parrish/Ludwig No. 727*

"Evening," House of Art, 1922. Large size, 15″ x 12″. *Parrish/Ludwig No. 665*

"Garden of Allah," House of Art, 1918. Originally designed for a Crane Chocolate gift box, the large size print measures 15″ x 30″. *Parrish/Ludwig No. 641*

"The Garden of Opportunity," Detroit Publishing Company, ca. 1915. Three murals of the Curtis Publishing Company included are (left to right): "Love's Pilgrimage," *Parrish/Ludwig No. 590*; "The Garden of Opportunity," *Parrish/Ludwig No. 611*; and "A Call to Joy," *Parrish/Ludwig No. 592*. Size: 24¼″ x 25″.

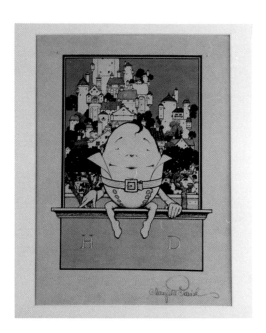

"Humpty Dumpty," a proof for L. Frank Baum's *Mother Goose in Prose*, 1897. Way and Williams produced a special collection of the fourteen proofs with each set being signed by the artist in pencil on the bottom margin. The edition was limited to twenty-seven sets. *Parrish/Ludwig No. 158*

"The Gardener," P.F. Collier & Son, 1907. *Parrish/Ludwig No. 426*

"Hilltop," House of Art, 1927. Medium size, 12″ x 20″. *Parrish/Ludwig No. 722*

"In the Mountains" art print, 1978. 20″ x 16″. *Parrish/Ludwig No. 745*

"The Lute Players," also called "Interlude," House of Art, 1924. Printed in a vertical version, 15″ X 12″, as well as a cropped horizontal version. Originally painted as a mural for the Eastman Theater, Rochester, New York. *Parrish/Ludwig No. 680*

"Jack Frost," P.F. Collier & Son, 1936. 12½″ x 13″. *Parrish/Ludwig No. 761*

"The Lute Players," House of Art, 1924. Large size, 18″ x 30″. *Parrish/Ludwig No. 680*

"The King of the Black Isles," P.F. Collier & Son, 1907. *Parrish/Ludwig No. 421*

"The Page" or "The Knave Watches Violetta Depart," House of Art, 1925. 9¾" x 12". *Parrish/Ludwig No. 713*

"Morning," House of Art, 1922. Large size, 15" x 12". *Parrish/Ludwig No. 672*

"Old King Cole," 6½" x 25". Dodge Publishing Company, 1906.
Parrish/Ludwig No. 568

"The Pied Piper," P.F. Collier & Son, 1909, printed by Dodge
Publishing Company. 6¾" x 21". *Parrish/Ludwig No. 505*

"The Prince" or "The Knave," House of Art, 1925. 10" x 12".
Parrish/Ludwig No. 709

"Pierrot's Serenade," art print with a poem from P.F. Collier & Son.
Image size 6½" x 4⅞". Also available in a 9½" x 11" art print.
Parrish/Ludwig No. 461

"Prince Codadad, His Brothers, and the Princess of Deryabar," P.F. Collier & Son, 1906. *Parrish/Ludwig No. 419*

"Dreaming" is the central portion of this large triptych with "Reveries" on the left and "Interlude" on the right. House of Art, 1928. *Parrish/Ludwig No. 727* (center), *No. 723* (left), *No. 680* (right)

"Romance," House of Art, 1925. According to Ludwig this was printed by Scribner's Press from the original plates of *The Knave of Hearts* for Reinthal and Newman. (*Parrish/Ludwig No. 696*) On the right "The Prince" or "The Knave," (*Parrish/Ludwig No. 709*), and on the left is "The Page" or "The Knave Watches Violetta Depart," *Parrish/Ludwig No. 713*

"Royal Gorge of the Colorado," 1925. Parrish gave permission to the Clark Equipment Company to publish the "Spirit of Transportation" without the trucks as an art print. According to Ludwig, when he saw it advertised under the name "Royal Gorge of the Colorado" he wrote to his publisher: "I was amused at the title...The tree was taken outside my studio window here [Vermont]; the brook was from the back of Windsor, the rocks were from Bellows Falls, and a mountain or two from Arizona. And yet I've heard some say they have been just to that spot." 20″ x 16½″. *Parrish/Ludwig No. 659*

"Sea Nymphs," P.F. Collier & Son, 1910. Published as part of the *American Art by American Artists* collection published by P.F. Collier in 1914. *Parrish/Ludwig No. 458*

"The Rubaiyat," House of Art, 1917. Large size, 8″ x 30″.
Parrish/Ludwig No. 620

"Sing a Song of Sixpence," P.F. Collier & Son, 1911, published by
Dodge Publishing Company. 9″ x 21″. *586*

"Spirit of Transportation," 1923. (*See "Royal Gorge of the Colorado."*)
659

"Stars," House of Art, 1926 or 1927. Large size, 18″ x 30″.
Parrish/Ludwig No. 720

"Sugar-Plum Tree," Charles Scribner's Sons, 1905. 16″ x 11″.
Parrish/Ludwig No. 552

"Sweet Nothings," detail from the Curtis Building murals. 19½″ x
10¼″. *Parrish/Ludwig No. 610*

"The Tempest: The Strong-Based Promitory" originally painted for Winthrop Ames's production of the Tempest in 1909. Parrish called the image "The Yellow Sands Outside the Cave." Published by Dodge Publishing Company. 7″ x 7″. *Parrish/Ludwig No. 502*

"Toyland" art print offered by Collier's. This image was originally used as a poster for the Toy Show and Christmas Present Bazaar, Madison Square Garden, December 18-26, 1908. That poster and this print were 28¼″ x 24″. *Parrish/Ludwig No. 479*

"The Valley." Originally appeared as the left half of a two-page illustration of "Ode to Autumn" in *Century Magazine*, November, 1904. *Parrish/Ludwig No. 385*

"Wild Geese," House of Art, 1924. 15″ x 12″. *Parrish/Ludwig No. 717*

"The Whispering Gallery," detail from the Curtis Building murals. 19½″ x 10¼″. *Parrish/Ludwig No. 609*

"With Trumpet and Drum," Charles Scribner's Sons, 1905. 16″ x 11″
Parrish/Ludwig No. 343

"Wynken, Blynken, and Nod," Charles Scribner's Sons, 1905. 16″ x
11″ *Parrish/Ludwig No. 342*

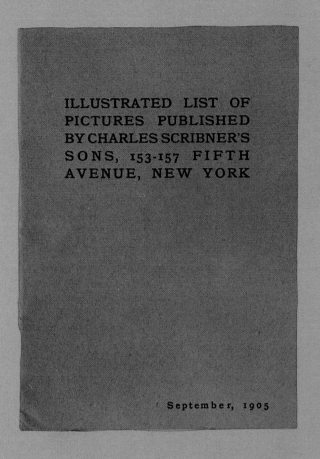

"Illustrated List of Pictures Published by Charles Scribner's Sons,"
September, 1905, featuring "The Dinkey-Bird" on the first page.
Parrish/Ludwig No. 378

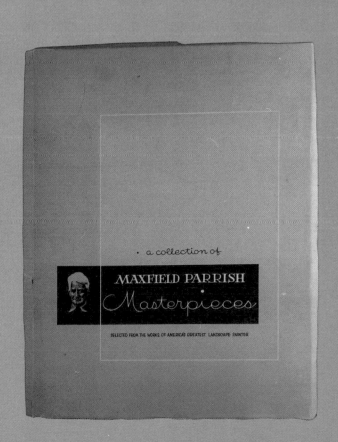

"A Collection of Maxfield Parrish Masterpieces." The spiral bound
calendar included "Evening," *Parrish/Ludwig No. 794*, "An Ancient
Tree," *Parrish/Ludwig No. 809*, "Sun-up," *Parrish/Ludwig No. 791*,
"Daybreak," *Parrish/Ludwig No. 807*, "Thy Rocks and Rills,"
Parrish/Ludwig No. 782, and "Evening Shadows," *Parrish/Ludwig
No. 823*.

"A Collection of Maxfield Parrish Masterpieces," Brown and
Bigelow, was issued as a bound calendar, 1956. This is the packaging.

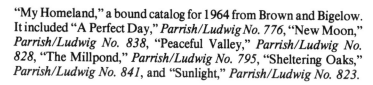

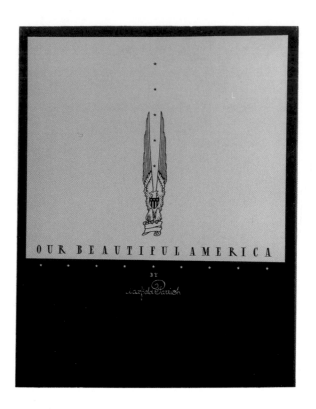

"My Homeland," a bound catalog for 1964 from Brown and Bigelow. It included "A Perfect Day," *Parrish/Ludwig No. 776*, "New Moon," *Parrish/Ludwig No. 838*, "Peaceful Valley," *Parrish/Ludwig No. 828*, "The Millpond," *Parrish/Ludwig No. 795*, "Sheltering Oaks," *Parrish/Ludwig No. 841*, and "Sunlight," *Parrish/Ludwig No. 823*.

"Our Beautiful America," four color reproductions from Brown and Bigelow, early 1940s. They included "Peaceful Valley," *Parrish/Ludwig No. 750*, "Twilight," *Parrish/Ludwig No. 758*, "The Village Brook," *Parrish/Ludwig No. 770*, and "Thy Templed Hills," *Parrish/Ludwig No. 760*.

"Maxfield Parrish's Four Best Paintings," P.F. Collier and Son. They included "Circe's Palace," *Parrish/Ludwig No. 448*, "The King of the Black Isles," *Parrish/Ludwig No. 421*, "Prince Codadad, His Brothers, and the Princess of Deryabar," *Parrish/Ludwig No. 419*, and "Cassim in the Cave of the Forty Thieves," *Parrish/Ludwig No. 413*.

Theatrical Designs

Parrish loved to tinker and build in his workshop, a fact of which nearly every early biographer made note. Some of the products of the workshop were models for theatrical sets. A few of these have entered the collectors market.

He also designed scenery for a production of Shakespeare's "The Tempest." An art print of one of these "An Odd Angle of the Isle" is included in the previous chapter. A less sophisticated design was made for the Plainfield, New Hampshire Town Hall theatre in 1917.

A model of the throne designed and built by Parrish for a Walter Wagner production of "Snow White." The show did not make it to the stage because of the onset of World War I. According to Ludwig, the models remained in the attic of Parrish's studio at the time of his death. *Parrish/Ludwig No. 623a*

Parrish's model of the barge for production of "Snow White." *Parrish/Ludwig No. 623b*

Around 1917 Parrish designed some woodland scenery and backdrop with a view of Mt. Ascutney for the town of Plainfield, New Hampshire. This old photograph on the cover of the town's 1961 annual report, is likely an image of that scenery. *Parrish/Ludwig No. 640*

BOOKPLATES

Larger rendition of the bookplate, measuring 10″ x 7½″.

Bookplate for John & Ethel Van Derlip in use. *Parrish/Ludwig No. not assigned.*

"Be Good—Ellen—Her Book" bookplate for Ellen Biddle Shipman, illustrated in *Century*, July 12, 1912. *Parrish/Ludwig No. 506*

The bookplate for *The Knave of Hearts. Parrish/Ludwig No. 697*

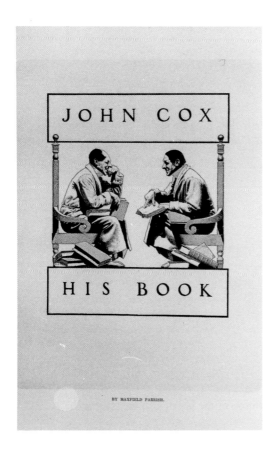

The John Cox of this bookplate did not exist. The bookplate appeared in *Century* magazine in an article entitled "The Appeal of the Bookplate," December, 1901. According to Ludwig, the name of Dean Sage was substituted when the bookplate was sold. *Parrish/Ludwig No. 296*

Miscellaneous Items

The variety of items on which Parrish images appear is great. Some of them are beyond categorization, except that of miscellaneous.

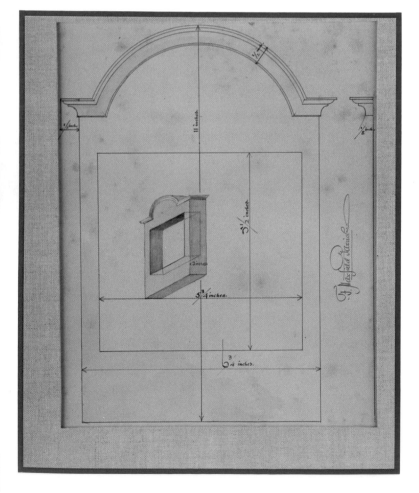

A clock case design by Maxfield circa 1890-1893. Measuring 11¾" x 9¼", it may be related to the clock face described in Ludwig as the first work ever exhibited by Parrish. It is signed "F. Maxfield Parrish." May be related to *Parrish/Ludwig No. 001.*

A letter on the back from Parrish's son, Maxfield Parrish, Jr., gives some more information.

> This working drawing...was made by my father...about 1890 to 1893, a time during which he was preoccupied with the design of baroque mantel clocks. He drew up many designs, and also made many of them in the carpentry and wood carving shop of George R. Shaw...

During this same period dad was also experimenting with various signatures. He thought Frederick Parrish was sort of plain, and Frederick Maxfield Parrish seemed overly long. He signed his F. Maxfield Parrish. In a few years, he dropped the F. and left it simply Maxfield Parrish, after his Grandmother's maiden name. She was a delightful person, and this choice was partly to honor her.

The drawing is dimensioned, and signed, so it is probably an acceptance sketch. He would not have signed a strictly in-studio working drawing.

Sketches attributed to Parrish, with certification by Alma Gilbert. Though unsigned they are believed to be some of the 41 drawings Parrish made for the entertainment of his children cataloged by Ludwig. If so they are *Parrish/Ludwig No. 578*

Copyright applications for "The Waterfall," dated February 18, 1930, filled out and signed in Parrish's hand. He describes the oil painting: "Two girls in shadow leaning over rock, in left foreground, watching a waterfall which pours down through a rocky ravine. Large tree on left. Effect is of late afternoon illuminating rocks & water in middle distance. Size: 31″ high x 22″ wide."

Copyright application with accompanying black and white image of the overmantel panel Parrish painted at the home of Philip S. Collins, Wyncote, Pennsylvania, 1920. *Parrish/Ludwig No. 655*

This illustration for A. Hensalt's "Berceuse" sheet music, was first used in the December, 1898 issue of *Century Magazine* to illustrate an poem called "Christmas Eve." The Century Library of Music; copyright 1901, by The University Society, Inc. *Parrish/Ludwig No. 205*

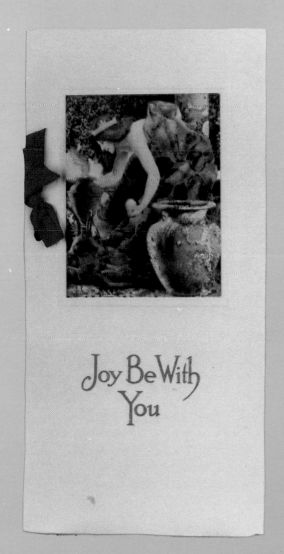

"The Wassail Bowl" decorates the cover of this book of sayings *Old Friends are Dearest* published in 1912 by Dodge Publishing Company. "The King of the Black Isles" (*Parrish/Ludwig No. 421*) is on the frontispiece. *Parrish/Ludwig No. 495*

Joy Be With You, a book of sayings featuring "Gulnare of the Sea" on the cover. *Parrish/Ludwig No. 418*

Color Advertising Salesman's book featuring Parrish's "The Pirate" on the cover. 11½″ x 16″. *Parrish/Ludwig No. 481*

Brochure for the Hotel Knickerbocker, New York, dated 1909. On the back is the image of "Old King Cole" with its dimensions, eight by thirty feet. Inside the brochure are photographs of the various rooms of the Knickerbocker, including the lounge where the painting hung.

Postcard featuring "The Pied Piper," *Parrish/Ludwig No. 505*

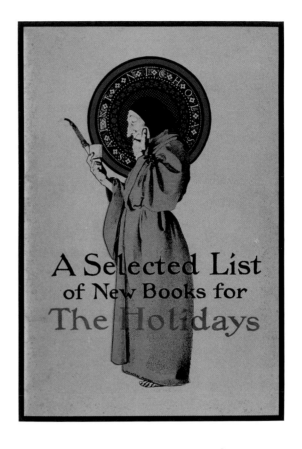

"St. Nicholas" adorns the cover of the brochure for Dodd, Mead, & Co.'s "New Books for the Holidays," 1917. *Parrish/Ludwig No. 215*

Parrish designed the cover of the pamphlet about his friend, Ethel Barrymore. *Parrish/Ludwig No. not assigned*

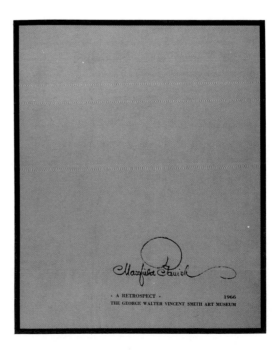

A retrospective exhibition of Parrish's work was mounted at the George Walter Vincent Smith Art Museum of Springfield, Massachusetts in 1966. This is the catalog from the exhibit.

Subscription card for Ladies Home Journal, c. 1912. From the Florentine Fete murals, "Buds Below the Roses." *Parrish/Ludwig No. 605*

Subscription card of for *The Saturday Evening Post* with "The Garden of Indolence," from the Curtis murals. *Parrish/Ludwig No. 613*

Advertising card for *Success Magazine* which has a four inch tall rendition of Parrish's December, 1901 cover at the right. *Parrish/Ludwig No. 301*

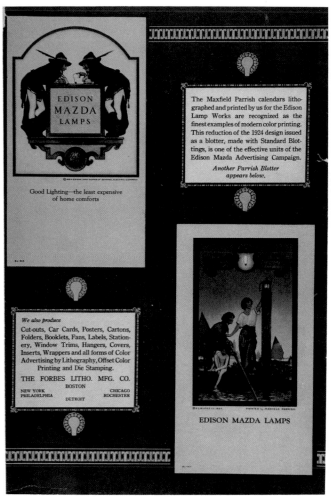

Forbes Litho advertisement featuring the Edison Mazda logo and the "Venetian Lamplighter." *Parrish/Ludwig No. 669 and 683*

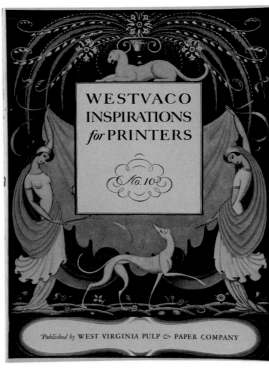

This card was called a "Printer's Inspiration" and was used to show the quality of work of the Westvaco Company. The outside is not Parrish, but the inside is identical to a subscription card for Ladies Home Journal, c. 1912, except for the black and white border treatment. From the Florentine Fete murals, "Buds Below the Roses." *Parrish/Ludwig No. 605*

Advertising folder for the Cook-Vivian Paper Co., with Parrish's *"Cinderella"* on the inside.

Thermometer decorated with *"Arizona,"* Thomas D. Murphy Co., early 1940s. *Parrish/Ludwig No. 739*

Thermometer with "Golden Hours," Thomas D. Murphy Co., early 1940s. *Parrish/Ludwig No. 726*

Tie rack with "Old King Cole," Pyraglass Co., 1909. *Parrish/Ludwig No. 568*

"Maxfield Parrish Soldier Ten Pens," Parker Brothers, Salem, Massachusetts, 1921. *Parrish/Ludwig No. 574*

"Toy Soldier" from a Parker Brothers children's game. The head detached when struck by a cork fired from a toy gun. 29½" x 15".
Parrish/Ludwig No. 574

"Comical Toy Soldiers and Gun," a cork-shooting game from Parker Brothers, 1921. In this game, the soldiers simply fell over when struck.
Parrish/Ludwig No. 574

General Electric Radio used this Parrish-esque figure in the late twenties. Here it is in two forms, a bandy doll, and a floor-standing ashtray. *Parrish/Ludwig No. not assigned*

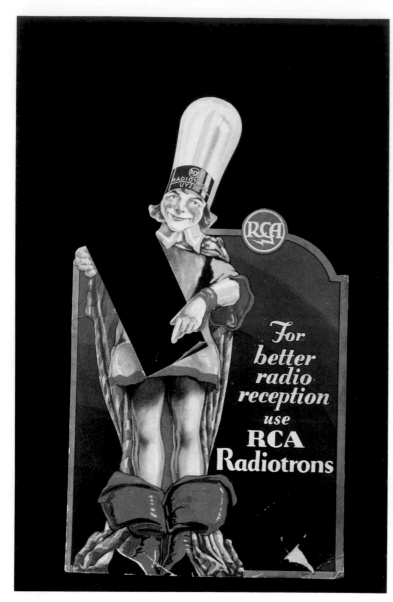

The design for this character for RCA Radiotrons is said to be of Parrish design, though it is not recorded by Ludwig. Die-cut cardboard, c. 1926.

The RCA character was also popular as a doll.

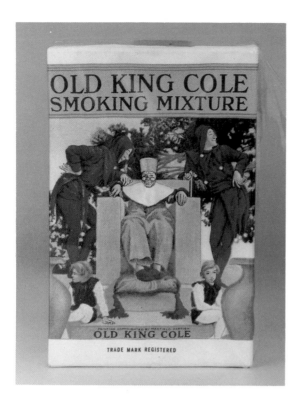

The image of Old King Cole which Parrish painted for the bar at the Hotel Knickerbocker in New York City was adopted for Old King Cole Smoking Mixture and Old King Cole Cigars. Here is the paper packaging for the smoking mixture. *Parrish/Ludwig No. 568*

Old King Cole Smoking Mixture tin. *Parrish/Ludwig No. 568*

Old King Cole cigar box label. *Parrish/Ludwig No. 568*

Bibliography

Bharucha, Fershid & Rosalie Gomes. *Buried Treasures: The Black-and-White Work of Maxfield Parrish, 1896-1905.* Petuluma, California: Pomegranate Artbooks, 1992.

Congdon-Martin, Douglas. *America for Sale: A Collector's Guide to Antique Advertising.* Atglen: Schiffer Publishing, Ltd., 1991.

Gilbert, Alma. *The Make Believe World of Maxfield Parrish and Sue Lewin.* Petaluma, California: Pomegranate Artbooks, 1990.

Holland, William R., Clifford P. Catania, and Nathan D. Isen. *Louis Icart: The Complete Etchings.* Atglen, Pennsylvania: Schiffer Publishing, Ltd., 1991.

Jackson, Denis C. *The Price & Identification Guide to: Maxfield Parrish.* Sequim, Washington: Denis C. Jackson, 1992.

Lane, Stephanie. *Maxfield Parrish: A Price Guide.* Gas City, Indiana: L-W Books Sales, 1993.

Ludwig, Coy. *Maxfield Parrish.* Atglen, Pennsylvania: Schiffer Publishing, Ltd., 1993.

Meyer, Susan E. *America's Great Illustrators.* New York: Harry N. Abrams, Inc., 1978.

Perry, Richard J. *The Maxfield Parrish Identification & Price Guide.* Portland, Oregon: Starbound Publishing Co., 1993.

Index

Parrish/Ludwig Number Index

A cross-reference to images appearing in this book by Parrish Ludwig Number and page.

Price
Guide

The prices in this guide are for Maxfield Parrish collectibles in fine to near mint condition - 8 or 9 on a scale of 1 to 10 - and for areas of average demand.

Expect to pay *higher* for pristine or uncirculated pieces, exceptionally ornate frames, items purchased on the West Coast and in other high demand areas, and rare items that seldom come on the market.

Expect lower prices for badly faded pieces, pieces that have been slightly trimmed or have minor foxing or creases, art prints in worn or non-original frames, and items purchased in low demand areas.

Expect substantially lower prices for pieces with holes, tears, bad foxing, major creases, water stains and major fading.

While the authors have tried to exercise all due care in developing this price guide, they are not responsible for any loss or gain experienced by those who use it.

BOOKS

Arabian Nights	100-125 (1st ed., 12 illus.)
	75-90 (2nd ed., 9 illus.)
Bolanyo	100-125
The Children's Book	50-75
Dream Days	100-125
Free to Serve	60-90
The Golden Age	100-125
Knave of Hearts	700-900 (hardbound)
	500-700 (spiral)
	100 extra for the box
Knickerbocker's History...	75-100
Mother Goose in Prose	800-1000
Poems of Childhood	200-250
Wonderbook and Tanglewood Tales	
	200-250
You and Your Work	50-75

MAGAZINES

Prices reflect minor wear, frayed edges, slight fading. Unframed. Values for internal pages are included when over $10.

American Agriculturist	100-125
Book Buyer	125-150 ea.
Book News	75-100 ea.
Century	Aug., 1917 cover, 100-125;
	Mar., 1905, "The Sandman," 50-75;
	full page internal illus., b&w, 10-15, color, 10-25
Collier's	3/4/05. 25-40;
	other covers, 50-75;
	full page internal illustrations, 20-40
The Critic	50-75
Everybody's Magazine	10-20
Harper's Bazar	Easter, 1895, 200-250;
	Mar., 1914, 100-125
Harper's Monthly	50-75 ea.
Harper's Round Table	
	4th of July, 1895, 125-150;
	Christmas, 1896, 125-150;
	Sept., 1898, 50-75
Harper's Weekly	12/08/00, 25-50;
	others, 75-125
Harper's Young People	75-125 ea.
Hearst's Magazine	100-150 ea.
Illus. London News	St. George, 50-75;
	At the Passing of Toys, 25-50
Ladies' Home Journal	
	June, 1896, 100-125;
	Sept., 1904, 100-125;
	July, 1912, 100-125;
	other covers, 50-75;
	internal full page illus. 15-35
Life	12/02/99, 125-150;
	12/01/00, 100-125;
	03/03/04, 75-100;

	02/02/05, 75-100;
	03/17/21, 75-100;
	10/13/21, 75-100;
	04/06/22, 75-100;
	03/29/23, 100-125;
	other covers, 50-80;
	internal full page illus., 15-35
Magazine of Light	150-200 ea.
McClure's	Nov., 1904, 75-100;
	Feb., 1905, 25-50;
	internal full page illus., 15-25
Mentor	Mar., 1922, internal full page illus., 10-20 ea.
Metropolitan Magazine	
	Jan., 1917, 100-125;
	internal full page illus., 10-20
Minneapolis Tribune-Picture	
	08/10/75, 10-20
Minnesota Journal of Education	50-75
New Hampshire Troubadour	50-75 ea.
New York Tribune	03/23/19, 25-50
New England Homestead	25-50
Progressive Farmer	50-75
Red Letter	50-75
St. Nicholas	
	internal full page illus., 10-25
Saturday Evening Post	
	Dec., 1974 article, 10-20
Scribner's Magazine	
	Aug., 1897, 50-75 (12 illus.);
	Dec., 1897, 100-225;
	Dec. 1898, 50-75 (15 illus.);
	Apr., 1899, 100-125;
	Oct., 1899, 75-100;
	Dec., 1899, 75-100;
	Aug., 1900, 10-20 (5 illus.);
	Oct., 1900, 75-100;
	Dec., 1900, 75-100;
	Aug., 1901, 25-50 (9 illus.);
	Dec., 1901, 50-75 (cover);
	Aug., 1923, 125-150.
Scribner's 1898 Prospectus	250-300
Scribner Christmas	
Dinner, 1897	250-350
Success	50-75
VIM	100-150
Yankee	25-50

COVERS AND PROGRAMS FOR NON-COMMERCIAL INSTITUTIONS

Haverford College covers	300-350 ea.
Mask & Wig Club program covers	
	350-450 ea.
Jefferson Theatre program	450-600

POSTERS

Adlake Camera	2000-2500
American Water Color Soc.,	200-2500
Book News	1200-2500 ea.
Century Midsummer Holiday	
	2000-2500
Century May, 1902	1000-1500
Colgate & Co.,	2000-2500
Davis Theatre,	400-600
Ferry, Peter, Peter	100-1200
Ferry, Jack	1200-1500
Peter Piper	1000-1200
Harper's Weekly	2000-2500
Los Angeles Municipal Arts	200-300
M-P Productions	50-75
Maxfield Parrish Museum	50-75
New Hampshire	600-900 ea.
No-To-Bac	poster, 1750-2000, post card, 100-150
Poster Show	200-2500
Red Cross poster set	1250-1500
Scribner's Fiction Number	200-2500
Christmas Scribner's	2000-2500
Scribner's April 1899	1250-1500

ADVERTISEMENTS

Brill Brothers	100-125
Broadmoor Hotel cookie tin,	300-400;
	advertisement, 15-25;

	brochure, 100-150
Colgate & Co.	advertisement, 15-30; calendar, 250-300
Crane	stamp, 50-75; chocolate box, 350-450 ea.
Curtis Publishing pamphlet	75-100
Djer-Kiss	window card, 300-400; magazine ad, 50-100; sheet music, 125-150
N.K. Fairbanks	35-60
Ferry Seed	small art print, 200-250; other ads, 20-40
Fisk Rubber	Modern Magic Shoes ad, 15-25;
	The Fisker, Sept., 1917, 200-300;
	Fit for a King ad, 15-30;
	Fit for a King display, 750-1000;
	Mother Goose ad., 15-30;
	wallpaper section, 200-250;
	art print, 300-450;
	Magic Circle ad, 15-25
Genesee Pure Food, Jell-O	
	ads, 15-40 ea.
Hire's ads	15-25 ea.
Oneida Community ad	15-25
Pettijohn ad	15-25
Royal ad	15-25 ea.
Swift Premium Ham ad	15-25
Tea Tray postcard	30-50 ea.
Vermont Association for	
Billboard Restriction poster,	600-800, postcard, 20-40
John Wanamaker catalog	250-350

CALENDARS AND GREETING CARDS

Brown & Bigelow produced calendars and greeting cards in many sizes from 1936-1963.

Greeting cards & desk-size calendars	15-30
Sm. calendars (8" x 11" cropped size)	
	1936-1956, $100-150;
	1957-1963, 80-125
Medium calendars (11" x 15")	
	1936-1956, 200-275,
	1957-1963, 150-225
Large calendars (16 1/2" x 22")	
	1936-1956, 300-450,
	1957-1963, 250-300
Extra large calendars	400-500
Playing cards	175-250 ea.
Winterscape executive prints,	
	200-250 ea.
P.F. Collier 1907 calendar	350-400
Dodge Publishing calendars	
	125-150 ea.

Cadmus Sowing...	125-150
Canyon	100-125 (sm.), 250-300 (lg.)
Cassim in the Cave...	100-125
Circe's Palace	100-125
Cleopatra	225-300 (sm.), 650-800 (med.), 1250-1500 (lg.)
Daybreak	50-75 (sm.), 150-225 (med.), 275-375 (lg.)
Dinkey Bird	150-200
Dreaming	100-135 (sm.), 240-325 (med.), 800-1000 (lg.)
Evening	100-125 (sm.), 200-250 (lg.)
Garden of Allah	75-100 (sm.), 150-200 (med.), 350-450 (lg.)
The Gardner	225-275
Hilltop	125-150 (sm.), 250-325 (med.), 800-1000 (lg.)
Humpty Dumpty	Rare
In the Mountains	25-50
Interlude	250-300
Jack Frost	200-225
The Lute Players	125-150 (sm.), 250-325 (med.), 500-600 (lg.)
King of the Black Isles	125-150
Morning	125-150 (sm.), 200-250 (lg.)
Old King Cole	150-225 (sm.), 800-1000 (lg.)
The Pied Piper	850-1100
Pierrot's Serenade	225-275
The Prince	200-250
Prince Codadad	100-125
Reveries	150-200 (sm.), 250-350 (lg.)
Romance	700-900
Royal Gorge of Colorado	500-600
Rubaiyat	75-100 (sm.), 250-300 (med.), 550-650 (lg.)
Sea Nymphs	225-275
Sing a Song of Sixpence	800-1000
Spirit of Transportation	650-800
Stars	200-225 (sm.), 650-750 (med.), 1200-1500 (lg.)
Sugar Plum Tree	200-250
Sweet Nothings	200-250
The Tempest	100-125
Toyland	1800-2000

Edison Mazda Calendars				
Year	Lg. Complete	Lg. Cropped	Sm. Complete	Sm. Cropped
1918	2500-3000	1000-1250	1000-1250	300-350
1919	2500-3000	1000-1250	1000-1250	300-250
1920	2500-3000	1000-1250	1200-1400	300-350
1921	2200-2500	1000-1250	900-1200	250-300
1922	2200-2500	1000-1250	1000-1250	300-350
1923	2000-2250	1000-1250	800-1000	250-300
1924	2000-2250	700-900	600-800	250-300
1925	2000-2250	800-1000	500-600	275-350
1926	2000-2250	800-1000	500-600	200-250
1927	1000-1250	600-700	450-550	175-225
1928	1500-1750	800=1000	500-600	200-250
1929	1000-1250	600-800	450-550	175-225
1930	2000-2250	800-1000	600-700	225-275
1931	2000-2250	800-1000	600-700	225-275
1932			450-550	200-250
1933	2000-2500	800-1000	600-800	225-275
1934			800-1000	225-275

Lighted Mazda tin sign	2500-3000
Enamel signs	1800-2500
Life-size cardboard sign	1800-2500
History of light, counter signs	600-800 ea.
Full page magazine ads	20-50
Edison Sales Builder	250-350 ea.
Blotter	50-75
Playing cards, 1918-1924	250-300

ART PRINTS

Aucussin Seeks Nicolette	350-400
Bellerophon Watching...	100-125
Broadmoor	100-125 (small), 400-450 (large)

impossible.	
p. 194: Knickerbocker Hotel brochure	
	100-150
p. 195: Pied Piper postcard	50-75
New Books for the Holidays	
	200-250
p. 196: Ladies' Home Journal	
subscription card	75-100
Saturday Evening Post	
subscription card	75-100
Ad for Success Magazine	175-250
p. 198: Cook-Vivian Paper Co. ad	
	150-200
Thermometers	100-125
p. 199: Tie rack	350-450
Ten Pins game	1250-1500
p. 200: Toy soldier game, complete	
	1000-1200
Comical Toy Soldiers gun game	
	1250-1500
p. 201: Jointed figure (top)	600-650
Ashtray (bottom)	800-1000
p. 202: RCA die cut sign (top)	500-700
RCA figure (bottom)	600-650
p. 203 Old King Cole paper package	
(top)	250-300
Tin (middle)	600-800
Cigar label (bottom)	50-75

Whispering Gallery	200-250
Wild Geese	225-275
With Trumpet and Drum	275-325
Wynken, Blynken, & Nod	300-350

OTHER THINGS

Items in the chapters on Theatrical Designs, Book Plates, and Miscellaneous Items are not all assigned values. Many are unique or rare. Some are pictured for the first time in this volume. Since they become available on the market so infrequently, pricing accuracy is

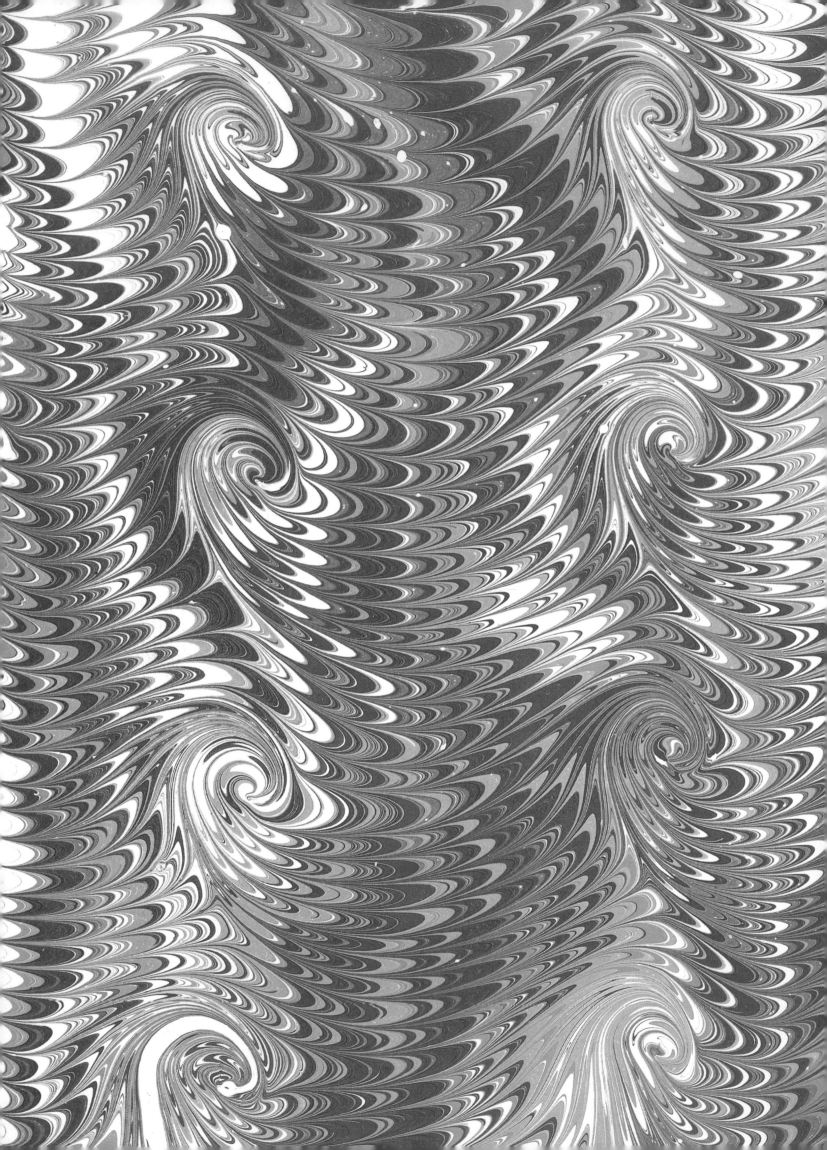